LAMBARENE

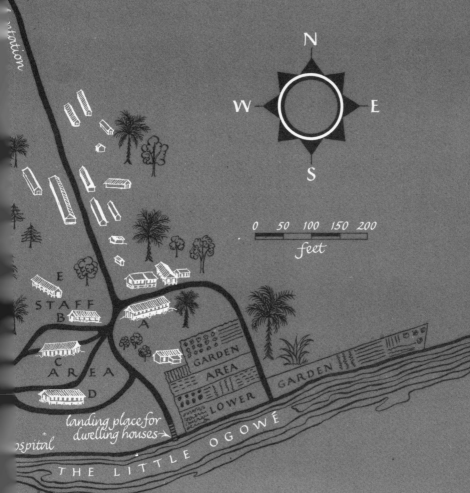

N
W · E
S

0   50   100   150   200
feet

STAFF

E
B
A
C
AREA
D

GARDEN
AREA
LOWER GARDEN

landing place for
dwelling houses →

hospital

THE LITTLE OGOWÉ

Home for doctors & nurses   E   European patients
European patients   F   Main hospital building
...ards, rooms for workers + orderlies, store rooms, etc.

The Africa of Albert Schweitzer

Dr. Schweitzer, with his St. Francis-like attachment to animals, has a special fondness for antelope fawns. Here he is with Léonie and Theodore. "Léonie knows when I've had a hard and hot day," he laughs. "See—she comes up and licks my arms dry. She likes the salt in the perspiration." His pet antelope fawns nuzzle the Doctor and chew his trousers. Léonie sniffs at the clothes of one of the American visitors. The Doctor chuckles, "She's too well educated to eat Boston trousers!"

The fawns are growing big, and it takes considerable strength now to restrain them as they tug on their leashes.

The Doctor recalls: "Léonie and her mother fell into a pit set by the *indigènes* to trap animals. When the natives arrived, the mother in her fright gave a mighty bound and leaped out, but the poor little fawn was left behind. The *indigènes* brought her to me, and I have raised her."

At sundown each day, the Doctor tries to pull himself away from the endless chores for a few minutes' relaxation with his fawns. He sits on the hill sloping down to the river and stares out reflectively through the palm trees and across the broad water. He cannot remain long, however, for the malaria-bearing anopheles mosquitoes come with the darkness and impose an automatic curfew.

the Africa of ALBERT SCHWEITZER

CHARLES R. JOY & MELVIN ARNOLD

with a concluding essay by ALBERT SCHWEITZER

PHOTOGRAPHS BY CHARLES R. JOY

HARPER & BROTHERS, NEW YORK

THE BEACON PRESS, BOSTON

Local Pronunciations

	PRONUNCIATION	MEANING
Adalinanongo	Ah-dah-lee-nah-nong-ge	Present site of Hospital
Andende	Ahn-den-day	First site of Hospital
brousse	bruhs	Country covered with bushes
bubu	bu-bu	Shirt
Galoas	Gah-loh-ah	Coastal tribes
indigènes	an-dee-zhen	French—native
Lambarene	Lawm-bah-ray-nay	District administrative center in French Equatorial Africa
Marecages	Mah-ray-kahzh	Marshy country near coast
negrier	nay-gree-ay	French—slave-trader
Ogowe	Oh-goh-way	African river
okoume	oh-ku-may	African tree
pagayeur	pah-gigh-yer	French—paddler
pagne	pahny (y as in yes)	Piece of cotton cloth used as a garment
Pahouins	Pah-u-an (French nasal in)	Interior tribes
pinasse	pee-nahs	French—motor boat
pirogue	pee-rohg	dug-out

48 - 9372

Contents

Preface

This book is the story of a pilgrimage. The pilgrimage started years ago, when Albert Schweitzer began to claim our attention as a thinker, as a spiritual teacher and as the exemplar of a new living ethics of love. It continued through the years in a careful study of his books and his work, his purposes and his personality. It found practical expression in the preparation of an anthology of his writings and the translation of other of his works, that the many to whom the name of this man was still unknown should have an opportunity to acquaint themselves with his life and thought, so significant for this generation. Our concern for the hospital led to correspondence with Dr. Schweitzer. The anthology gave birth to a resolve to complete the pilgrimage by a visit to Lambarene in French Equatorial Africa where the Hospital had been built.

So it was that, one day toward the end of May, 1947, two of us—one a relief administrator and the other a book publisher—flew across the Atlantic and over the equator to Leopoldville in the Belgian Congo. The flight took a little less than two days. From that point on the journey into the heart of Gabon took a whole week by train and truck and finally by dugout.

On the seventh of June we shook hands with Dr. Schweitzer among the palm trees at his landing. The weeks that we spent at Lambarene were among the most memorable of our lives. We were not mere spectators of a miracle of mercy. We were generously admitted as members of the Hospital family. We walked and talked, ate and worked, with Albert Schweitzer. We were assigned our little portion of the responsibility. We were permitted to share the problems, the anxieties, the hopes, the plans, the dreams of this extraordinary jungle doctor.

Few have been able to enjoy that experience. The journey to Lambarene is long, costly and arduous. That such a privilege was ours places upon us a heavy responsibility. This book represents part of our effort to discharge it. The Schweitzer Hospital is the Doctor's personal enterprise. It is wholly autonomous, dependent on and supported by no mission or foundation. If it is to continue into the distant future, it must be better known, and the spirit of its founder must be maintained. The authors of this book have tried to preserve here and to share with others the image so clearly engraved upon their memories, the picture of a rare personality quietly engaged upon a humble but immensely significant task, and supported by a staff filled with the greatness of his spirit. We want others, too, to know this man and his helpers, and the work that is their duty to perform.

In the midst of busy lives this book has slowly taken form. It was planned and begun at Lambarene. It was continued in Paris, in London and at the Doctor's own Alsatian home in Günsbach. It has traveled over three continents. It has visited a score of countries. Five times it has flown the Atlantic, four times it has spanned the American continent.

It is now presented, pictures and text alike, as a humble tribute of affection and esteem for one who has learned some of the secrets of life's beauty and truth, one who has tried to build firm foundations for the city of God in the deep, black, virgin soil of humanity.

C. J.

M. A.

Boston, Massachusetts,
June, 1948

NOTE: to avoid awkwardness in the text, the first person singular pronoun is used to indicate either or both of the authors. The photographs are by Dr. Joy

AFTER A THIRD OF A CENTURY ON THE OGOWE

The "Prisoner of Lambarene" stares reflectively down the Ogowe toward the spot, two miles downstream, where he landed in 1913. There, the philosopher-theologian-musician-physician began his work of mercy. Dr. Schweitzer says, "The work is more desperately needed now than when I came here a third of a century ago. The diseases introduced by the white men take a rising toll. The people's habits of life are changing, and they must be helped and guided."

For a third of a century, Dr. Schweitzer and the staff of the Lambarene Hospital have lived and worked among *indigènes* who belong to the early days of man's history. There are many tribes, but in the main there are only two kinds of natives in the region. Those of the forest live the harder life. They have little sun and little air, their food is scarce and danger is everywhere. The natives of the plain find life much easier, and so they are simpler and more hospitable. They love noise, and song, and dancing. They can work hard when they want to, paddling upstream against a swift, strong current; carrying heavy burdens on their heads; but life on the whole is fairly easy for them. What we call civilization has hardly touched the native either for good or for ill. He lives in an earlier epoch of the world.

The "Prisoner of Lambarene"

The world is still young at Lambarene. River and sky and forest—
they have been there for long millennia—unchanged. The little fish
in schools see no danger as they glide down the stream. But the
pelican stands behind the rock waiting. Over the water at the edge
of a sandbank a stork stands on his long stilts. He, too, is fishing. Where the
river meets the shore, lovely flowers in yellow and rose return the sun's greeting.
Parrots fly overhead, their broad tails spread out like a fan. Monkeys chatter as
they swing from branch to branch high in the giant trees.

Lambarene stands at the center of a network of rivers, the highways of Africa;
but all around it is the jungle, black and mysterious. A few native trails, hidden
under the tall trees and rife with peril, penetrate the jungle, but it is largely
inchoate and unknown. Where it is still virgin, towering mahogany trees, kapoks
and okoumes cut off the sun from the earth, and there is little undergrowth. Only
where the high trees have been cut does the secondary forest grow dense and
impenetrable.

Here at Lambarene the earth still steams as in the earliest days. The nearness
of the equator, only forty miles away, makes the night and day approximately
equal the year around, and there are only two seasons, the wet and the dry.
The dry season is cooler than the wet, and the wet season is sunnier than the
dry. The torrential rains come usually at night, and during the day the earth gives
off its vapor under the incandescence of the sun. The heat is oppressive, the
humidity high.

I am sitting on the stone steps that lead to the lower garden in Lambarene,
here in the heart of this primeval world. To the right, tender plants just set out
are protected from the parching heat of a merciless sun by palm branches stuck
in the soil. Only yesterday these branches were cut from the top of the oil palms
under my direction, but already they are beginning to wither. To the left, the
men are turning the soil, the soil which is always red here in this country
because of the iron in the earth. Beyond the breadfruit tree I can see the huge
kapok that marks the end of the garden, and behind it the graceful palms of
Atadi. A growth of tall reeds separates the garden from the swift-flowing Ogowe,

THE WORLD IS STILL YOUNG AT LAMBARENE

The world is still young at Lambarene and still unfinished. A tangle of waterways merges with a tangle of forest, but where the river ends and the jungle begins no one can tell. The little tributaries lose themselves among the trees. Groves of papyrus spread their feathery foliage over the water, and endless morasses with their slimy, dripping muck defy the surveyor's rod and line, as they ooze into the streams. The great river, the Ogowe, stretches for hundreds of miles into the interior. The cumulus clouds of the sky are mirrored in the flood. In the distance it is difficult to determine what is cloud, what is water and what is the dull blue of the low mountain range. Downstream the river flows for more than a hundred miles to the sea, over huge, flat garden terraces. By the coast it becomes a delta. There the streams and the marshes and the islands form a great carpet pattern, fringed with the surf of the sea. Toward the north the marshes dry, and the gray-green changes to gray-brown. The waste is no longer a swamp. It is now a desert.

As this photograph was being taken, with the camera pointed upstream from Dr. Schweitzer's canoe, the "Clipper," he exclaimed:

"From the creation of the world—forest, river, clouds, like this!"

FROM VILLAGES SUCH AS THIS COME THOSE WHO BEAR THE MARK OF PAIN

In Equatorial Africa no one escapes disease and pain. Until Dr. Schweitzer came and established his Hospital, the sick and the lame in a wide area had no one to turn to but their native medicine men. Now, some five thousand men, women and children come each year to the Hospital—traveling by boat and on foot. They come from villages such as this in a great circle four to five hundred miles in diameter.

A typical village is made up of a half-dozen to two dozen shelters of the kind seen above. Each family lives in a one-room hut, made of mud bricks or of thin poles, covered with grasses and leaves.

In more advanced villages, however, the practice is growing of building houses that consist of two small rooms with an open, roofed-over corridor between, so that children may be separated from the adults.

The traveler in Equatorial Africa sees hundreds of such drab little primitive villages. There the native lives, working only enough to get sufficient to eat, and enjoying sleep as much as possible. Away from his little community, however, he grows homesick. One of the doctors at the Schweitzer Hospital asked a man recovering from an operation how he was. The man replied "My body is well, but my heart speaks of my village."

its green-brown waters reflecting the white clouds of a brilliant blue sky. Behind me are a few hundred acres of cleared land, covered with the buildings of a jungle hospital, and the orchards necessary to sustain it. Beyond that is the jungle again.

On the steps beside me sits quietly a big man with a shock of unruly, graying hair, and a thick, drooping mustache. He is stooped a little. Out of his square face, intelligent, penetrating eyes gaze over this peaceful scene. There is a far-off, tender look in them. One can see that this man loves what he sees. This is his country, these people are his people. He is dressed in the simplest fashion. An old sun helmet, covered with white cloth, is pushed back from his forehead. His white shirt is open at the neck, its pocket bulging with letters. His large muscular arms are bare. The khaki trousers are patched and darned. He sits quietly without speaking. The afternoon is drawing on, and he is taking a bit of repose.

In the heart of the forest a tam-tam sounds. It starts and stops in varying rhythms, speaking a language of its own. Off in another direction another answers—more slowly, more regularly. The forest is having a palaver. The big man lifts his head and listens. His beneficent influence has blessed the lives of natives for hundreds of miles around; yet he, too, is a stranger in this world of black primitives. He does not know the language of the drums. Neither he nor any other white man knows much of what goes on behind the dark veil of the forest. The white world is still as far removed from the black world in which it has taken root as is the brilliant sun of the rivers and marshes from the deep shadows of the jungle.

The big man sitting there beside me with his strong hands resting on his knees is Albert Schweitzer. Out of the forest he has carved a little patriarchy, which he rules wisely and gently. This around him is his village. This is his Hospital in the "brousse."

Dr. Schweitzer rules the Hospital, but it is equally true that the Hospital rules him. Once in his study-bedroom he remarked with a smile, pointing to the strong crossbars of the screened windows, "You see, I am a prisoner." The words have a profound meaning. Albert Schweitzer is the prisoner of Lambarene.

TO THIS HAVEN ON THE RIVER THEY TRAVEL

This is journey's end for the suffering. There, under the trees on the right bank of the Ogowe, they find the buildings that make up the Schweitzer Hospital at Lambarene in the Gabon region of French Equatorial Africa. Immediately above the Hospital, the river divides into two branches. The branch seen in the photograph is called "Orembo," which means "Little" River.

A third of a century ago, patients had to be wheedled into trusting themselves to the care of the white-skinned Doctor. Today they travel for days and even weeks to consult him. The Hospital is so much a part of the region that its existence is taken for granted—except by the witch doctors who resent the competition. The patients live in a world of nature, where they help themselves to nature's bounty; and the Schweitzer Hospital is accepted as part of the natural order. This means that seldom is gratitude expressed by a patient whose pains have been quieted or whose life has been saved. But this does not lessen the staff's earnest willingness to help. Says one doctor, "We are not here to be thanked for our work. The work itself is its own reward. At first I thought it would be a sacrifice to come here, but I no longer feel that way. We came to heal, and to heal we stay."

CROCODILES AND SHARKS AND ELECTRIC FISHES

Now the Ogowe is drowning its banks; in a few weeks, with the onset of the summer dry season, the river will go down, and the pirogues will have to be carried over bars of sand. That is when the crocodiles, dreaded as much as any creature on land or water, will shake off their winter lethargy and begin thrashing around the banks.

The river, like the equatorial forest, teems with life. We asked Dr. Schweitzer what kind of fish are to be found in the waters, and he replied, "I have seen sharks right here at our landing. (I fed one to my hens.) And swordfish with a sword a meter long. Then there are electric fishes. I re-member a young Englishman, named Noel Gillespie, who had been entrusted to me by his mother, and I felt particularly responsible for him. One day two other men—one a Swiss missionary twenty-four years old—and he went on a picnic to a lake in the vicinity. I made one condition in speaking to the Swiss missionary, that Noel should not go bathing in the lake. But they did not heed me. They all went swimming from the boat. The Swiss, who was the last in the water, suddenly gave a cry, threw up his hands, waved them frantically above the water and sank. The natives said he had been attacked by electric fishes."

"TZEH, POBA-HOBA; TZEH, TZUT, TZUT . . ."

On Sundays, as shown above, the Ogowe is splashed from bank to bank with the paddles of the dugouts. The craft are so stable that there is little danger of upsets even if the paddlers row while standing. Enterprising natives have even developed dugout taxi services. From the neighborhood of the Schweitzer Hospital, on either side of the river, they carry a native to the mission on Big Island for the equivalent of three cents. A European pays five.

The native workmen chant in unison when they are paddling or when a group wants to "heave ho" a heavy object, as in raising the ramp to a truck-ferry when it reaches the bank. Among the more popular chants are: "Yah-nyeh, yah-nyeh, yah-nyeh —yneeeeeeen-yah!" and "Tzeh, poba-hoba, tzeh, tzut-tzut; tzeh, poba-hoba, tzeh, tzut-tzut!"

When members of the Hospital staff make a pirogue trip of any length they provide the paddlers with a generous supply of their basic foods—bananas, manioc sticks, and palm oil. But during the trip the paddlers will stop and say they can't go on because they're hungry. What they mean is that they are hungry for meat or fish, and they want to see if they can persuade the travelers to give them extra money to buy some *viande* or *poisson* at the next village.

A River, a Doctor and a Hospital

Quan N'Yin, the Chinese god of motherhood, has a thousand arms. Albert Schweitzer's Hospital, also, has a thousand arms, and the arms are the jungle waterways. His Hospital had to be on the bank of a stream, for there were no roads, either of dirt or of steel, to lead into the interior of the continent. He established the Hospital at the heart of the great Ogowe River system, whose many branches were the arteries through which the life-giving blood of knowledge and healing and love flowed to the native villages. Without these rivers the Hospital could not have been.

In fact the early history of all central Africa is the story of great rivers and the men—such as Livingstone, Stanley and Brazza—who braved the hidden dangers to ferret out the secrets of the dark, unfriendly world drained by these surging streams.

From the time of the earliest explorers at the end of the fifteenth century, most of the expeditions brought with them priests, who established missions among the natives. Yet these early missionaries had little success because of the iniquities of the slave trade which quickly sprang up in the coastal areas. Upon this trade the *négriers* and those they worked for prospered. Even more shameful was the fact that the natives of the marécages and the savannahs near the shore co-operated with the slavers, so that the latter seldom had to gather their own human chattel. When their ships anchored off that long green coast, the slaves were already herded there waiting for them. The coastal tribes had hunted and captured them by means of forays into the interior. So the Dutch, Portuguese, Spanish, English, French and American traffickers and planters grew rich, while even the Christian churches defended this buying and selling of stolen souls. The slaves were baptized en masse, and pious preachers in distant lands rejoiced that these dark-skinned, thick-lipped people were now Christian slaves rather than free pagans.

In fairness to the church it should be remembered that early Christianity with its eschatological views had not condemned slavery. With the advent of the Messianic kingdom slavery would soon come to an end anyway. Therefore the existence of slavery was of no great importance. Paul simply accepted it as a fact; thus later Christianity lacked the authority of the early church in fighting the terrible institution.

The figures of the American slave trade are startling and ghastly. In order that 5,565,000 human beings might be transported to the Americas, 10,200,000 are said to have died on endless jungle trails, in crowded detention camps, in the rotten holds of vessels.

When the American preaching station was established at Andende in 1874, about two hundred miles upstream on a branch of the Ogowe River, the slave trade with America, which had flourished during the eighteenth century and the first half of the nineteenth century, had been stamped out by the vigilance of the English and French cruisers. In the interior, however, it still existed. The different tribes warred with one another to procure slaves which they sold to the tribes of the coast. The plantations around Lambarene were still worked by slaves. At that time the area around Andende marked roughly the boundary between the coastal Galoa tribes, and the tribes of the interior who belonged to the race of Fans, or Pahouins. The Pahouins were still a cannibal people. Terrorizing the more peaceful tribes, they continued to push farther and farther westward, until the mission station was surrounded by them, and the Galoas had withdrawn toward the sea. The coastal tribes would have been entirely destroyed had not the French government taken possession of the territory and put an end to the tribal warfare.

Into this region the traders and the missionaries came, only to encounter suspicion, hostility, privation and meager initial success. On what is now known as the American Hill at Andende, the first American Presbyterian missionary, Dr. John Nassau, built his house in 1876. It was a steep twenty-minute climb through the jungle to the top, from which a glorious view up the broad river spread out. It was not, however, for the view that the house was built. It was for safety from hostile and cruel natives, who dared not penetrate the jungle at night, but who were still able to make life miserable for this devoted pastor.

The last of the American missionaries was a Mr. Ford. When the French colonial authorities ruled in 1892 that all instruction in the mission schools must be given in French, the Americans withdrew in favor of the Paris Missionary Society.

It was to Andende that Albert Schweitzer came in April, 1913, with his bride and his brand new medical degree to begin his career in the tropical jungle. He was no young doctor, however, with his whole life before him. Dr. Schweitzer had already made his mark in three vocations. He was known in many lands as a thoughtful philosopher, a daring theologian, a distinguished musician and a brilliant writer. In the old-world village of Kaysersberg he had been born, on January 14, 1875. He was only a few months old when he was taken from the building, where his father preached in a humble little chapel and where the pastor's family also had its home, to the village of Günsbach in the neighboring valley of Münster, which spread out in broad meadows between the Alsatian hills. There his boyhood was spent in a parsonage with a large family, and there his ideals and central thoughts took abiding form.

The peculiar endowment of his nature set him apart from his time and his companions. When the other boys went hunting in the forests or when they went fishing in the little river Fecht he could not join them. Already his heart of compassion was open to the birds of the fields, to the fish of the stream, to the beasts of burden, to all creatures which like him were trying to enjoy their brief span of life. His heart went out to them. His childish prayers ascended on their behalf.

He was never a gay boy. At Mülhausen, where he later attended the lycée, the pastor who taught religion called him Isaac, which in Hebrew means "the laughing one"; but the pastor and the other teachers who complained because he was always bursting into laughter during the class periods little knew the reason for his apparent gaiety. The reason was that he had an irresistible sense of humor; his comrades, knowing this, exploited it to make him laugh, so that he would be reprimanded by his teachers. Yet inwardly he was a serious, thoughtful boy, which again set him apart from his companions. Perhaps exaggerating a little, he remarked in later years that he had never known as a child a completely carefree moment. In any case life quickly became for him a very serious, though wonderful, business. He was not a good scholar during his early years. He was too much of a dreamer. But toward the age of twelve years he seemed to come to himself and became a conscientious and careful student, although he never desired to excel.

So keenly did he feel his oneness with his comrades that he would not dress differently from them. This caused scenes and difficulties with the family, since he was a son of the village presbytère, but he persisted in his refusal to wear leather shoes when the other boys wore wooden sabots, or to protect his fingers in the winter while other boys wore fingerless mittens. He could not even enjoy the food spread on the parsonage table, knowing that other boys in the village were not so well fed.

At a very early age he tried to give expression to his spiritual life in poetry and in painting, but he soon gave them up, convinced that he had no aptitude for them. In music, however, he quickly found a congenial home for his spirit. When he first heard two-part singing in the Günsbach school, he almost fainted with the thrill of the harmony. The old square piano of the parsonage was his first instrument. At nine years he was playing the organ in the high loft of the village church, watching in the mirror above his head the pastor in the high pulpit at the other end of the church. At sixteen years he was occasionally substituting for his first great teacher, Eugen Münch, on the fine organ where Münch played, at St. Stephen's in Mülhausen. Because the boy at first preferred to improvise rather than study the lessons given him, Eugen Münch called him for a time "his nightmare," his "thorn in the flesh." But suddenly the boy found himself; soon he was playing Beethoven and Bach with a passion and sensitiveness that amazed and delighted his gifted teacher, to whom, untimely dead, he rendered later his tribute of living gratitude.

So in these earliest days his character was formed. It is not necessary here to outline in detail the brilliant career that opened before him. He pursued his studies at the University of Strassburg, at Paris and at Berlin. He was a Doctor of Philosophy at the age of twenty-four, with an important and independent study of Kant's philosophy of religion behind him. At twenty-six he published a book on the Last Supper which won him the degree of Licentiate in Theology, and gave him the right to become *Privatdocent* at the University of Strassburg. At thirty-one he published a remarkable book on J. S. Bach and his works. The following year he published a study of all the books that had to do with the life of Jesus, and in the same year a book on organ construction. Five years later he published a study of all the books that had to do with the interpretation of Paul's theology. At thirty-eight he was a Doctor of Medicine. A master now in four major fields of learning and a skillful writer as well, he was in demand everywhere as a lecturer, as a preacher, as an organ recitalist, as an expert consultant in organ construction.

Already the major decision of his life had been taken. At the age of twenty-one he had decided to devote his life to theology, philosophy and music until he was thirty, and thereafter to give himself to some direct service of mankind. At thirty while in Paris he dropped a letter into a mail box on the Avenue de la Grande Armée announcing to his family and his friends that he had decided to resign from his pastorate and from the directorship of the theological seminary at Strassburg, to devote himself to the study of medicine that he might go to Africa as a doctor to the natives. His friends were shocked. They could not understand. "The general does not go to the front with a rifle," said Charles Marie Widor. But Albert Schweitzer had decided. There followed eight years of pitiless study, when night and day he attempted to complete his medical courses, while at the same time continuing his writing, his music, his former intellectual interests. Only the extraordinary vigor of his constitution enabled him to finish his course just before the last ounce of strength was gone.

This, then, was the man who appeared at the station of the Paris Missionary Society on the Ogowe River, already a world-renowned figure, to work for the dark-skinned people of Africa. One of his first acts, after his arrival, was to write to Dr. Nassau, the old American missionary, that the mission station founded by him once again had a physician. Dr. Nassau replied expressing his great joy at the news.

1913: AT THE FOOT OF AMERICAN HILL

Here began Dr. Schweitzer's African career. It was this Protestant mission, founded by Dr. John Nassau at the foot of American Hill, that took him in and gave him space. Three times the natives had burned down Dr. Nassau's home and stolen his books (which are still found in widely-scattered villages). Finally, he built his home atop the hill, where he could more effectively stand siege. His sheer survival against such odds convinced many a native that God must be more powerful than their own N'Zame; they began attending the church. The foundation stones at the right are all that remain of Dr. Nassau's home.

HERE THE YOUNG DOCTOR BEGAN HIS HEALING

This is the building that was turned over to Dr. Schweitzer by the Protestant mission in 1913. Today the house is crumbling, but it is still used as a residence by the head teacher of the mission school on the riverbank below.

In Dr. Schweitzer's early years on the Ogowe, he and Mrs. Schweitzer used various rooms of this building for living space, office, pharmacy and consultations.

When the Schweitzers began work, supplies had to be stored in part on shelves in the living room; patients had to be treated in the open air under the hot, equatorial sun, and, when the usual evening rains of the hot season began, under the veranda of the dwelling. This, of course, could not continue long, and so an old hen house was converted into a hospital. There were no windows, and holes in the roof made it necessary to wear a tropical helmet even indoors—but at least it was an improvement over the open air.

The Schweitzers' first interpreter and native assistant, a man from the Galoa tribe, was called Joseph. That Joseph had previously been a cook was evident by his description of the pains described by the patients: "This woman has a pain in her upper left cutlet." "This man has an ache in his loin."

The story of the Hospital he started is an epic in itself. He had raised all the funds for the new enterprise. He had himself gathered all the supplies necessary for the establishment of the Hospital, seventy cases of them, all carefully classified and personally conducted through the mazes of transport and customs. When he arrived at this new post of service, his bungalow was waiting on the top of the little slope that rose from the river's edge, made gay with palms and flowers and paper lanterns; to the bungalow he and his wife were conducted triumphantly by singing natives rejoicing in the fact that the long-expected doctor had come at last to help them with their ills.

At that moment the brief romance of the adventure ended and the hard and drab labor of it began. Even before the chests of medical supplies were available, the sick people came, and there was nothing to use for them except a few things brought in the Doctor's trunk.

So the work began under the most primitive conditions. "Oganga" was the name given the Doctor by the Galoas. They had no other name for a physician: he was the fetisher, with power not only to cure disease, but also to cause it. A few months later Oganga was able to leave his hen house and move into a new building that had finally been erected with two small rooms for consultations and operations and two still tinier rooms for dispensary and sterilizations. By the end of the year two small buildings were ready, a waiting room for patients, and a dormitory for the ill. Approximately two thousand patients had passed through the Hospital, and as, by rare good fortune, all the operations were successful the reputation of the white fetisher spread far and wide. The initial difficulties had been overcome, the Hospital was established, and the Doctor was feeling the first joy of a dream realized.

Then on August 4, 1914, came an ominous word from Cape Lopez: "In Europe they are mobilizing and probably already at war." Christmas came, and when the candles on the little palm had burned down half their length, the Doctor blew them out. "They are all we have," he said. "We must keep them for next year." Not everyone was so pessimistic about the prospects as the Doctor. Many thought the war would be a short one. But the Doctor had to be prepared. He laid in a store of new supplies in readiness for all emergencies. Well it was that he did so, since the war was to prove long and disastrous. The natives were puzzled by it. "Why don't all the tribes get together in a palaver and settle things?" asked an old Pahouin.

A second wartime Christmas came, and the half-burned candles guttered in their sockets on the little palm tree. There were no candles for the third Christmas, in 1916, and still the war was not over. Food became scarce. They learned to eat strange meat at Lambarene. The work of the Hospital had now largely ceased. The Doctor, being an Alsatian, had been forbidden to practice, and he was even interned by a short-sighted government. This enforced leisure was used to good advantage, however. He had now the opportunity of spending days on end at his writing instead of at his Hospital, and so he began work on *The Philosophy of Civilization*. Later the rule against his Hospital activities was relaxed and he began to practice again. But just as he was resuming his routine duties the order came that he, among other prisoners of war, was to be transferred to Europe for internment there.

After a few weeks in temporary barracks at Bordeaux, where the Doctor developed a bad case of dysentery, they were taken to a great internment camp at Garaison in the Pyrenees.

In March of the following year the Alsatians were transferred to S. Rémy de Provence, where Dr. Schweitzer was puzzled by the familiarity of the bare and ugly rooms of another old monastery, until he suddenly remembered that he had seen them in a painting by Vincent van Gogh. For here it was that the artist had been confined as a mental patient.

About the middle of July an exchange of prisoners was arranged, and the Schweitzers were informed that they would be permitted to return home by way of Switzerland. It was fortunate, indeed, for both of them were ill. They found their way to Strassburg, and then by special permission back to Günsbach. Here in the little town—fortunately so concealed among the hills that it had not been destroyed by the war—the Doctor's chills and fevers and torturing pains grew worse until it was necessary to undergo an operation at Strassburg.

His recovery was followed by many activities. He accepted a position as physician in the municipal hospital. He was appointed once more curate at St. Nicholas. He worked on the study of the world religions. In 1920 he delivered lectures at the University of Upsala in Sweden, and then, encouraged by Archbishop Soderblom—like himself a simple, unconventional, but dominating character—he raised money to pay off the heavy Hospital debts by organ recitals and lectures throughout the country. Heartened by this kindly reception in Sweden and strengthened by the healthful climate, he made up his mind at last to return to Lambarene as soon as possible. For some time, however, it was not possible. Other journeys had to be made for the purpose of raising money for the Hospital expenses. The first two volumes of *The Philosophy of Civilization* and his book, *On the Edge of the Primeval Forest*, were finished and published; his books, *Christianity and World Religions* and *Memoirs of Childhood and Youth* were prepared for the press. Then on February 14, 1924, he finally left Strassburg to return to Lambarene.

How different was this journey! His wife did not accompany him now. She was too ill to return. It had been seven years since he had left the Hospital, and when at last at sunrise of the day before Easter he saw the mission station again, he found his Hospital buildings in a frightful state of decay. The building of corrugated iron remained, and the hardwood framework of one other building.

Everything else had decayed and collapsed. It was like starting again from the beginning; yet on Easter Monday the sick were there clamoring for treatment. The weeds and the creepers were cleared away, the roofs repaired and the fallen buildings rebuilt. It was an exhausting labor. In the morning Dr. Schweitzer worked as a physician, in the afternoon he worked as a carpenter and a mason. The work grew in magnitude. Two more doctors and two nurses arrived from Europe. By the autumn of 1925 the Hospital had been rebuilt and reorganized.

Then when it looked as if the strain were over, and when some leisure for his writing was in sight, a severe famine set in, accompanied by an epidemic of dysentery. The Doctor was in a state of almost complete despair. He had been so proud of the reconstructed Hospital, and now, as desperately ill patients flocked to it in unprecedented numbers, it was evident not only that the Hospital was totally inadequate, but that it could never be made adequate on that site. On all sides it was surrounded by the river, the swamp and the hills. There were ample quarters for fifty patients, but there were now one hundred and fifty to care for. There was no way of isolating the dysentery cases, there was no place for mental patients. Sick at heart at the prospect, and yet compelled by inexorable necessity, he decided that the Hospital must be constructed on a new and more spacious site.

At once he thought of a new location, the former residence of the old Sun King, N'Kombe, a broad hilltop three miles upstream from Andende. An application to the District Commissioner quickly brought a grant of land, 172 acres of it, on the sole condition that it be built on or cultivated. The decision to move the Hospital, to build it for the third time, was communicated to the staff; and the work began. Dr. Schweitzer's wife and child had expected to see him back in Europe in the winter of 1925-26, but now his return had to be postponed for long months to come. The work of construction had to be carried out under the Doctor's immediate supervision. Each morning, the available workers, usually about fifteen, were rounded up and transported to the new site. There the work of clearing the land was undertaken, and a garden and plantation prepared. It often took several days to cut down one of the huge trees, and after it was cut it took more days to saw it into sections and dispose of it. As many as possible were spared for shade.

At the beginning of 1927, when the short dry season came, the first removals took place. This meant not only the removal of patients, but at the same time the removal of furniture and supplies, the shifting of all the old planks and beams. All day long Dr. Schweitzer was on the river towing pirogues full of supplies, furniture, planks and patients. It was a frightful task, but at last it was over; and from all the new wards there came the happy, enheartening comments, "This is a good hut, Doctor, this is a good hut!" In the old Hospital, floors had been of damp earth, and the rooms had been dark and stifling. In the new Hospital, the floors were of wood, and the buildings were well ventilated and lighted. There was still much to be done, but the major task was completed. There was now room for 250 patients and their attendants. There were proper isolation wards for dysentery, eight cells for the mental patients. On July 21, 1927, Dr. Schweitzer left for Europe, the great task of removal and reconstruction finished. But there was pain in his heart as the low green strip of coast faded from sight behind him. "It seems to me incomprehensible," he wrote, "that I am leaving the natives for months. How fond of them one becomes, in spite of all the trouble they give one." Africa had become for him a second home.

As a matter of fact he was to be away from the natives for a considerable time during the next ten years. He made long trips to Europe whenever it was possible to leave the Hospital in capable hands. He returned to Lambarene whenever his presence there seemed necessary. There were lectures and concert tours in Sweden, Denmark, Holland, Germany, Switzerland, England and Czechoslovakia. In 1928 he received the Goethe Prize from the city of Frankfort, delivering an address there on his indebtedness to Goethe. With the twenty thousand marks he received he built a home in Günsbach for himself and for the personnel of his Hospital while on leave in Europe. But his conscience troubled him, and so by concerts and lectures he raised another twenty thousand marks for German charities and missions. He kept the simple little house of a story and a half on the edge of the Black Forest village of Königsfeld, for his wife's health demanded occasional sojourns in high altitudes, and he greatly admired the spirit of the Moravian Brethren (Herrenhuter), whose establishment dominated the town.

In 1932 he returned to Frankfort to speak again on Goethe, this time on the one hundredth anniversary of Goethe's death. There were Hibbert Lectures at Manchester College, Oxford, on "Religion in Modern Civilization," a series afterward repeated at London University College. There were two courses of Gifford Lectures in Edinburgh. In rapid succession appeared important books from the pen of this tireless writer: *The Mysticism of St. Paul, Out of My Life and Thought, The Forest Hospital at Lambarene, Indian Thought and Its Development* and *From My African Notebook.* Intermittently, also, he worked on the final volume of *The Philosophy of Civilization,* which he planned to call *Reverence for Life.*

These manifold activities in Europe were not completely divorced from Hospital activities, however. The Hospital had to be supported. It was Doctor Schweitzer who raised most of the money for it, lecturing frequently on his work and its needs.

In February, 1937, he returned for his sixth sojourn in Africa. During the preceding ten years the Hospital had continued to grow, increasing the number of its buildings, expanding its beneficent service. To the first group of buildings on the new site others had been added. The Necklace Building was named for an

SITE NUMBER TWO FOR THE SCHWEITZER HOSPITAL

In the mid-1920's, it became obvious that the original site of the Hospital would be inadequate. Dr. Schweitzer began the search for a long stretch of riverbank that would allow for the expansion of the Hospital buildings. He investigated the area once occupied by the old village of Adolinanongo, which had been abandoned in 1883 when the inhabitants had moved to the other side of the river to protect themselves from the invading Pahouins. The jungle had repossessed the land, but oil palms showed that men had once lived there, and the forest was young. There was a little valley near the river, easy of access from the water, and on slightly higher ground where the native village had stood was spacious land for the white quarters. With two of the natives Dr. Schweitzer explored the site, cutting paths with ax and machete through the jungle.

Slowly the jungle growth was hacked back from the shore, and today, scattered under the great palms, are forty structures, ranging from the main Hospital building and ward buildings down to a shed for dugout canoes. Now 110 acres are cleared out of a total of 220. Scores of acres are under cultivation. It is more than a hospital in the Western sense; it is a community of three to four hundred patients and staff members.

G. H. Q.: FIRST FOR THE SUN KING; NOW FOR THE DOCTOR

This is the Doctor's headquarters: his small combination study-office-bedroom is at the end of the long, narrow building. Adjoining it is the narrow room into which are jammed his piano with its organ pedals, his books and the wire enclosure for his pet antelopes. The other rooms in the building are occupied by Mrs. Schweitzer, staff members or used for storage. The compound on which the building is located was formerly the site of the crude palace of the Sun King of the native tribes.

At Lambarene Dr. Schweitzer has become, as he himself says, "a modern prehistoric man." His Hospital has been built like a lake dweller's village on piles— so that high river waters will not endanger the buildings and so that the torrential rains of the long wet season may sweep down from the hillside without carrying them away.

When construction of the new Hospital was begun in 1926, the storeroom was the first building to be completed, in order that the tools might be stored safely on the site. Next was the main Hospital building, then the surgical ward, eighty feet long and sixteen feet wide. Then came a building for the Pahouins, another for the Galoas, another for the Koulou-Moutou tribe—so that each could have its required isolation.

English lady who sold her necklace to raise the money for it. The Emmy Hopf Building was named for an organist in Berne who gave concerts for it. A building for mental patients was given by the Guild House in London. A maternity ward resulted from lectures given by Mlle. Gertrud Koch, one of the Doctor's nurses. A building called the "River House" was erected with gifts from the Misses Mary and Alice Christian and Mrs. Emilie Rieder, all three from London. Even the cistern was a memorial building. A building for the lepers, a dining room and other buildings were completed. "The Doctor's Village" had been erected.

The mighty forces of decay which he had so vividly described in the first volume of his philosophy were at work, however, in Europe; when he arrived there in early February, 1939, he decided that the war he had feared was inevitable, and that for him the post of duty was at Lambarene. With a heavy heart he returned to Africa on the very ship that had brought him to Europe, arriving March 3. At every port along the way there were warships; talk of fighting was in the air and on the lips of everyone. There was no time to spare.

The next few months were spent in a feverish effort to prepare for the imminent conflict. Medicines were purchased in Africa and ordered from Europe. Large quantities of rice were laid in as food reserves. The staff was readied for the coming emergency. Fortunately most of the supplies arrived from Europe either before or immediately after the beginning of the war. The last shipment of drugs and surgical supplies went down with the steamship "Brazza" when it was torpedoed off Cape Finisterre.

With the actual outbreak of the war a sad decision had to be taken. All of the sick except those critically ill and those in need of emergency operations were sent home. The limited resources of the Hospital had to be conserved. By the little river steamers, by the motor boats, by the rude pirogues and by the lonely forest trails, the natives that had arrived with such hope returned to their villages in disappointment. Even to distant Africa the war had quickly come.

This was indeed evident when the forces of Vichy and the forces of Free France fought over the little village of Lambarene in the fall of 1940. The Hospital, fortunately, was situated about two miles up the river· from the town, and the planes of both sides spared the buildings. But there were many stray bullets; the staff protected themselves as best they could by placing sheets of galvanized iron against the sides of the houses, and by taking refuge behind the thick concrete walls of the emptied water cistern. The strife ended in the victory of General de Gaulle's men, and thenceforth the fate of French Equatorial Africa was bound up with the fate of the Allies. This meant that relations with Europe became very difficult, while relations with England and America remained relatively open.

The work of the Hospital continued on a diminished scale. Some of the nurses found employment elsewhere, so that only four of them remained. The medical work was carried on by Dr. Schweitzer and by his competent assistants, Dr. Ladislas Goldschmid and Dr. Anna Wildikann. Mrs. Schweitzer, who had managed somehow to travel from France to Lambarene by way of the Portuguese colony of Angola in the summer of 1941, helped greatly in many ways. In the middle of 1942 the shelves in the pharmacy began to show great empty spaces; but almost by miracle arrived new stores of drugs and new pledges of assistance from America. They had been more than a year on the way. Later came precious shipments from England also.

There were many changes in the personnel of the Hospital. The climate was very hard on many Europeans. Some of them could not endure it for more than a short time. But the hardier members of the staff remained in spite of increasing weariness and expanding work.

After the first period of war retrenchment, it was possible and necessary to enlarge the work again. It was possible because of gifts of medicines and money from America and England. It was necessary because of the large increase in the number of white patients. They, too, had grown weak and anemic from their prolonged sojourn in the tropics. Their diet lacked calcium. They had ulcers of the stomach from the use of palm oil, which seems to be harmful to the whites. They suffered from deep muscular abscesses. They had malaria. Fortunately the Hospital never lacked the drugs necessary for the treatment of these ailments.

There was no radio at the Hospital, and it was only by a brief semi-weekly bulletin from Lambarene that the devoted staff heard of the war in Europe. On Monday, May 7, 1945, Dr. Schweitzer was sitting at his study table after the noonday meal, writing letters that had to be despatched by two o'clock that afternoon on the downstream boat. A sick European, who had brought a radio to the Hospital with him, suddenly appeared before his window with the news that, according to a German communiqué, relayed by the broadcasting station at Léopoldville in the Belgian Congo, an armistice had been concluded in Europe. Another man would have jumped from his table to carry the news to others, to join in some impromptu celebration. Not so Dr. Schweitzer! There was work to be done, which neither war nor peace must interrupt. He finished his letters in time for the steamer. He descended to the Hospital where his heart patients were waiting for him. Only after that ministration was at an end did he have the bell of the Hospital sounded and the announcement made that the war in Europe had come to a close. Even then, tired with the labor of the day and the deep emotional strain, he dragged his feet up to the plantation to see that the work there was progressing properly.

FOR PROTECTION FROM THE SUN AND FROM WILD ANIMALS

The Doctor pioneered, in this part of the tropics, the type of building shown in these views of the Hospital grounds. The structures are long and narrow, on an east-west axis, so that the sun never hits them broadside. Formerly the houses of Europeans were big and square, and there was little ventilation through the inner rooms. Under the Schweitzer plan, every room has direct cross-ventilation; and there is a long air channel under the roof, connecting all the rooms. For some reason, the Europeans persisted—and many still persist—in cutting down the trees where they built. The Doctor not only preserved the trees, for shade, but planted new ones where needed. As a result, the buildings of the Schweitzer Hospital are several degrees cooler than the other buildings in the district.

The Schweitzer Hospital is set down in the middle of wild-game territory. This is the reason the windows and doors of the buildings have heavy wooden bars. The forest is alive with gorillas, elephants, panthers and other creatures. One evening, while the Doctor was working at his table, he heard a soft scuffle at his door. He looked up and found himself staring into the eyes of a full-grown panther. From time to time, natives mauled by wild beasts are brought to the Hospital.

Corridor between two staff barracks, with late-afternoon sun.

A general view of the lower Hospital grounds—patients' quarters.

Dormitory building for several staff members and for European patients.

Barrack-type building for members of the *indigène* staff.

Dining hall for the staff, with one guest room in the corner.

The thick cover of trees gives day-long protection from the sun.

HIS CAPITAL: WIVES AND DAUGHTERS

This village chief, like most of the men in the region of the Schweitzer Hospital, has more than one wife. Wives and daughters are his capital. The forest is free; his home costs nothing but a few days' labor; there are no banks. So when a native husband acquires a little extra cash, he puts it to work by investing in another wife. When he gets hard up, he can sell a daughter—or even a wife. But the wife or daughter does not resent being bought and sold.

Because of the heavy burden of labor on the women they frequently nag their husbands to have plural wives. In nearly every district of huge Equatorial Africa,

polygamy is practiced. It is almost impossible to stamp out. There are powerful economic and social forces that compel it. Even many a missionary is convinced that polygamy cannot be abolished independently of other social and economic factors.

Romance, in the Western sense, is unknown. The sharing of intimacies is taken casually. Boys and girls begin relations at fifteen or sixteen years, and there is no stigma of juvenile delinquency. No one frowns when a girl has a child. This makes her all the more desirable as a future wife because she has proved herself in the field where a woman is most highly prized.

The Struggle of Equatorial Africa

In the Lambarene Hospital we see in miniature the great drama that is taking place in all of Equatorial Africa, the drama brought about by the juxtaposition and intermingling of a primitive and half-primitive material and spiritual culture with one that is modern. The foreign culture of the whites makes its influence felt in many spheres and in many ways; the primitive culture of the natives often withdraws before it. Yet the primitive culture does not succumb: it continues to exist beside and in contrast to the foreign culture. Consequently there have arisen a mingling and a juxtaposition, an interpenetration and an opposition, of which one can gain some notion only through personal experience.

The native is immersed in a primitive world. This world is partly concealed by a coating of certain European views and customs. In its principal features, however, it has kept its identity. The natives of the older generations were able to yield to the higher spiritual traditions of the whites. This is no longer true of the natives to the same extent. They accept much, particularly whatever is useful for their daily life; but nonetheless, with certain exceptions, their lives and feelings—so far as their fundamental convictions are concerned—are determined by primitive, inherited views.

Polygamy is something that is taken for granted. This is true also of blood vengeance, which so often leads to murder and poisoning—although the natives possess a kind of good nature which is expressed in a lack of ordinary vindictiveness.

Ideas of magic permeate their thinking. The belief that men can enter into relations with supernatural powers in mysterious rites, and so share in supernatural faculties and powers, they never completely abandon. The conviction that men can inflict injury upon others by magic, so that they sicken and even die, continues to be widely held, causing terrible acts of vengeance upon those who are thought to be guilty and upon their relatives. The belief that men can be so completely at the mercy of the spiritual power others possess over them that they are compelled to do whatever they are bidden—however irrational and frightful it may be—can produce in poor blacks who come under the influence of sinister personalities the delusion that they must regard themselves as leopards in human form, and as such must creep up on and kill their own relatives and friends whenever these are pointed out to them as victims.

The idea of taboo is also deeply rooted in the thought of the natives, so that a man his whole life long has to accept as his destiny whatever his parents or relatives at his birth—on the inspiration of the moment—proclaimed as absolutely binding upon him. A man's taboo might be that he may not eat out of a vessel in which bananas have been cooked, without suffering the penalty of death. Another must be careful never to get the slightest blow on the head, because this also would mean his immediate death.

With many natives the taboo is so powerful that when—knowingly or unknowingly—they sin against their taboo they actually suffer what was foretold for such a contingency, or fall seriously ill. Dr. Schweitzer's assistants told us of several such cases. It is sometimes possible to deliver these poor people from their tormenting taboos. A Protestant missionary, M. Lavignotte, spends much time doing this; thanks to his penetrating knowledge of the mind of the native he has already been able to help several of them.

We were impressed with the fact that, for the native, the blessing of a man as well as his curse has real significance. (This idea is also to be found in the Old Testament.) In consequence of native notions about blessings, it is supposed to be significant when a child receives the name of another person, if this person has been asked and has given his consent. So it happens sometimes that a white person who has a good reputation is asked if his name may be given to a child. The name becomes in this way the child's possession. A blessing, then, goes forth from the white person to accompany the child throughout his life.

In giving names, the natives now and then behave in a very extraordinary fashion. Not infrequently does it happen that boys have girls' names and vice versa. A mother who has lost her first boy through death, or who has a taboo that the son she will bear will meet with ill fortune, may hit upon the idea of giving the newborn boy a girl's name. In this way he discards the other sex, so to speak, and wards off the ill fortune that threatens his actual sex.

The idea that a woman must not consent to give her breast to a nursing child whose mother has died brings misfortune on many black children. A woman who takes over the mother's responsibilities toward the child becomes in a certain degree its mother, and is therefore in danger of meeting the same fate as the actual mother. Since cows cannot live in the jungle because of the tsetse fly, since goats also are seldom found, since people are usually not in a position to procure milk for the motherless child, it is permitted to starve. If a woman in defiance of superstition should have compassion upon the child and wish to nurse it, she would be prevented from doing so by her family, since such conduct on her part might bring bad luck upon her own children. Formerly thousands of motherless children in the jungle were condemned to death. Nowadays, whenever the natives know that canned milk is available at the mission stations, they bring the poor little creatures there so that they may be brought up on the bottle. A number of such children are usually to be found in Dr. Schweitzer's Hospital also. Every possible effort is made to prevail upon the grandmother or the aunt who has brought the child to remain with it in order to protect and care for it. The effort does not always succeed. Thus it may happen that the nurse who cares for the babies has a number of them entirely dependent upon her—sometimes an almost intolerable burden.

For three years such children are kept in the Hospital. Anyone entering the consultation room in the morning is greeted by the many-tongued crying of the nursing babies who lie or sit around in the boxes and baskets in which they have been brought. It may be noon before the nurse who takes care of them—with the help of the black orderly, Gaston—has finished washing and caring for them. The doctors and nurses who are busy in the same room are so accustomed to the tumult that they are no longer bothered by it. There are certain good reasons why the consultation room should also be the place where the bottle-fed babies are cared for; in particular, this gives the doctors the advantage of having the children constantly under their eyes and being aware of their progress.

Under the influence of Christianity, native women have sometimes been induced to assume the responsibility of kinship toward the orphan nurslings. These cases, however, continue to be exceptional.

Evil Spirits exert a fearful dominance in the life of the natives, who take it for granted that nature as a whole is peopled with Spirits that can bring misfortune upon men. Spirits that wish him well and do him good do not seem to be assumed.

There are Spirits above all in the forest. A native dreads being alone in the forest, not only because of the wild beasts, but also because of the Spirits. He does his best to avoid being in the forest at night—something easy to understand by anyone who has experienced the mystery of the jungle in the darkness.

Especially terrifying are the spirits of the dead. According to primitive belief, the spirit of a man leaves his body at death and wanders restlessly about in the neighborhood, with power to molest and harm members of the family. In order to keep these spirits as far as possible from the village, the natives bury the dead without ceremony in some lonely spot in the jungle. From the whites they have learned of cemeteries in which the dead of a community are all buried together. They have not yet proceeded to lay out cemeteries in the neighborhood of their villages, but they have gone so far as to want to bury their dead on some piece of land that has been cleared of forest and presumably will remain so. The villages in the vicinity make use of the Hospital cemetery. Even when they are not Christians the relatives often request someone from

THE WIVES' SERVITUDE IS BALANCED BY EXTRAORDINARY FREEDOMS

Equatorial Africa is, in many respects, a woman's world, to a degree not even dreamed of by the suffragists of the Western world. Dr. Schweitzer chuckles when he tells of members of his audiences, on his lecture tours, expressing horror at the servitude of the native women. In some areas of life there is servitude; but in other areas the women are more free than civilized women. In general terms—economically, they are in servitude; socially, they are free.

The woman does have to provide the fruits and roots for the family. The husband's responsibility for these foods is that, every three years, he must clear a few acres of forest for his wife (or wives) to plant, cultivate and harvest. This must be repeated every so often because the bananas, a basic crop, exhaust the soil. The husband sees his task as that of slashing down the brush and trees, and then burning them in the summer dry season. If, as occasionally happens, the rains continue through the summer, and the brush will not burn, then he and the other men and their families resign themselves to famine. Of course, he could slash the brush and trees into small sections so they could be dragged to one side of the clearing and heaped up. But that is unthinkable labor. The Evil Powers are frowning, and

starvation is to be accepted. Thousands of natives were lost after the long wet seasons of 1925 and 1934. Many others survived only because Dr. Schweitzer had been able to gather together some funds and had accumulated large stores of rice.

The wives tramp out to the plantations and laboriously tend the crops. Some plantations are necessarily so far from the villages that the women stay there for days before returning, sleeping in crude little shelters on the edges of the clearings.

To compensate for her heavy economic burdens, the *indigène* wife has important compensations. She is free to travel at will—many wives spend three or four months a year visiting friends and relatives in other villages. Also, after a baby is born the wife is a free woman. So long as the baby is nursing, the husband may not touch the wife. ("That would poison the milk.") The native mother usually nurses her child for between a year and a half and two years.

In many districts, the new mother is expected to go home to her native village, if she is from another settlement, and spend the whole two years with her own family. Even though the children belong to the mother's family, and not to the father, it is the father who receives the cash payments when daughters are sold.

the Hospital to conduct simple services. They remain faithful to the old custom, however, that people from the village of the dead should not accompany the body. Only the bearers and a few men of the family are present. Women take no part in the interment, even when it is a woman who is being committed to the earth.

The real ritual for the dead takes place in the village after a number of weeks. Then the people of the village and the guests who come from a distance are entertained; for two or three entire nights, dances with a ceremonial meaning take place accompanied by the tam-tam, by singing and shouting. This joyous festival, which often becomes quite wild, bears the name of the "lifting of sorrow." It means that the spirit of the dead is now no longer wandering about, but has been laid to rest by the ceremonies underlying the dances.

Dr. Schweitzer has made it a rule that the dancing and tam-tam beating should come to an end by ten o'clock in the evening in the villages in the neighborhood of the Hospital. He has great difficulties, however, in seeing that this rule is observed. The natives are opposed to this rule, maintaining that an entire night is necessary for the performance of the ceremonies.

The fundamental meaning of this ritual, which involves a great deal of noise, is simply that the spirit of the dead is driven away from the village, so that there is nothing more to fear from it.

The conviction that noise has some power over every kind of Spirit lies behind the custom of hanging bells at the bow of the dugouts that traverse stretches of dangerous rapids. The vibration produced by the powerful strokes of the paddles causes a constant ringing. This continuous noise is supposed to drive away the Spirits that might bring danger in the rapids to the dugout and its crew.

The trials by ordeal contrived by the fetishers play a great part in Equatorial Africa. During the ordeal, the accused is given a drink which will not harm him if he is innocent, but which will kill him if he is guilty. The drink is prepared from bark or roots containing poison. The fetisher, of course, completely controls the outcome of the ordeal. If he puts only a little of the poisonous bark or roots into the water, or none at all, the accused will not be harmed by drinking it. If he prepares it in such a way that it contains a great deal of poison, then of course the accused is condemned. There may be cases in which the fetisher prepares the drink according to the judgment he has formed as to the guilt or the innocence of the accused in the case. For the most part, however, he acts capriciously or in accordance with bribes he has been given to find the accused guilty or innocent. "You may believe me," said Dr. Schweitzer, "that among those who accompany a sick person to the Hospital someone is often found who does not belong to the family; he comes under compulsion, not willingly, because he is suspected of having produced the illness by the practice of magic. The members of the family watch over him very carefully and prevent his escape. If the sick man dies he is brought before the fetisher and forced to drink the ordeal cup."

The trial by ordeal is often used in cases of sudden death, for it is readily believed that these are caused by magic.

The horrible practice of the ordeal, together with many other evils of the region, must, in Dr. Schweitzer's judgment, have their roots torn up. The roots are the inherited superstitions of these primitive people. The missionaries of all confessions co-operate with each other in endeavoring to do this. Only when the native can be brought to lift himself above the superstitious ideas in which he is imprisoned does he really emerge from his primitive environment.

"And we should not think," declares Dr. Schweitzer, "that the natives will be freed from the old superstitions only through the knowledge they gain in the schools. Experience teaches that this is not true to the extent that we might expect. Very often those who on the basis of their general education pass as 'intellectuals' are in a very special way attached to the old superstitions and the institutions associated with them."

In many respects something like a renaissance of magic is taking place among the natives today. It is somewhat similar to the revival of the old Greco-Oriental mysteries in the first three centuries of the Christian period. Just as at that time certain cults and conceptions, which seemingly could not continue to exist beside the world view formulated by the great Greek thinkers, nonetheless took on new meaning and found new expression—so today the primitive and magical world view of the colonial peoples maintains its place beside the thoughtful and ethical world view that they have come to know through the Europeans. Secret societies in which the old views and cults continue to be practiced find new adherents in the new generations. Magical ideas demand recognition as the highest ideas beside and above the knowledge based on reason.

In justification for clinging to the old magic the natives could point to the continuance of superstition among the whites—and they do not fail to do so. They learn of the whites' superstition through newspaper advertisements of fortune tellers, and through publications that deal with astrology. Astrological studios from different lands send series of printed letters to the natives asking them to send money for the valuable disclosures concerning their activities and their fate revealed by astrology.

The whites who play with superstition in this fashion, or who exploit it for commercial reasons, share responsibility for the fact that the present generation of natives has been strengthened in its belief in magic, which causes so much misery among them and which interrupts their spiritual development. These whites hinder the educational work that must be carried on among the colonial peoples.

"YOU CAN'T ORDER ME AROUND! . . ."

A girl, like the young Galoas above, is normally sold on the installment plan. A boy, after a few years of carefree promiscuity, will decide to start earning money to buy a wife—partly so that he will be able to sell the daughters he hopes to have. He goes to work in a timber concession, or gets a job in town, and starts saving. The paymaster-nurse at the Schweitzer Hospital keeps out part of the wages each month for those boys who want help in accumulating a wife-purchase fund. Sometimes a Hospital workman will decide the strain is too much, ask for his horde and squander it.

The young husband makes his down payment of cash, and adds a sheep or a goat, some cloth and a machete; then pays, say, an equal sum of cash next year, and the following year. He's under the impression he has completed his installments, because he feels he remembers something about a total price of about $25 in cash and the various gifts in kind. But no; he is mistaken. The wife's family distinctly remembers that another $5 is due —and immediately. Something of this sort happened while we were at the Schweitzer Hospital. One of the medical aides, in great agitation, went to a nurse and asked to be permitted to go to the village downriver at once. One of his wife's brothers

had just come and demanded payment of 100 colonial francs ($1.50) for his wife. If it were not paid on the spot, the brother would take the wife back (a perfectly legal procedure). The aide did not have the 100 francs, and the Hospital has learned that to advance such sums would be an open invitation to the family of nearly every wife on the place to discover additional installments due. So, disconsolately, the husband went down the river, and spent half the night in a palaver with the family; he finally agreed to pay the $1.50, but persuaded the family to let him have until payday to deliver it.

The wives don't mind being bought on the time-payment plan, nor do they mind the way their families contrive to keep installments falling due almost endlessly. So long as the wife is not completely paid for, her natural independence is even heightened. ("You can't order *me* around —you haven't even paid for me yet!")

Not only can the wife be taken back to her family—often spirited away in the night—but also she can be reclaimed by the family if the husband maltreats her. If the wife decides her husband is being unfairly harsh or demanding, she merely has to send word to her family. Her brothers or other villagers will steal into the hut at night and take her back.

GAUDY COTTONS FROM LANCASHIRE EASE WIFELY BURDENS AT HOME

Dr. Schweitzer and other observers have found that the native women are essentially happy. Even their duties in the plantations are being offset by a decline in the crafts that formerly occupied their time. Where, formerly, the native woman would prepare raffia and weave crude garments, she now insists that her husband buy rainbow-hued cotton from Lancashire and elsewhere. He can't object, because usually he himself has taken to wearing cotton trousers and perhaps a shirt, instead of the old raffia or cloth wrap-around. As for the wife, she certainly isn't going to be seen in the village dressed in an old-fashioned, drab reed garment if her husband is sporting modern trousers and perhaps even a felt hat or a sun helmet of the kind the white man uses. This adoption of the white man's dress is due partly to a desire to be in fashion and partly to superstition. Many a native is convinced that, when he has on Western clothes, the Evil Powers that are searching for him will take a quick look, say, "That's a white man," and continue their hunt. The trading posts in the region are kept stocked with cottons of a dazzling variety. Among the women in the larger centers, the custom is growing of wearing cotton scarves or kerchiefs on their heads, while the back-country women go bare-headed.

ENVIED MOTHER WHO LOST ONE DAUGHTER TO POISONING

This woman, possessing a natural dignity that would be envied by many a European, is an example of those few natives who are able and willing to embrace Western civilization while living in a primitive society. She is the wife of a young missionary, who himself is the son of a respected native pastor. She has had six children—all daughters. Five are now living. The sixth? Poisoned. The Schweitzer Hospital staff believe she was poisoned out of jealousy by one or more of the other wives in the woman's village. It was just too much for them to stand—that this young wife could outrage the village gods by becoming Christian, and then have the unbelievable good fortune to give birth, consecutively, to six healthy, vigorous daughters. The young family has had other difficulties, for the father contracted leprosy. Fortunately, he underwent treatment promptly at the Schweitzer Hospital, and is now virtually cured. The staff of the Hospital is fond of the family, and welcomes the parents and children when they return for physical check-ups or for treatment of the minor ailments that afflict every family. On this visit, only three of the children had the adventure of a trip to Lambarene with their mother, while the other two stayed home with their hard-working father.

NO ROOM FOR ORIGINALITY IN HAIR-DO's

When the Westerner first enters Equatorial Africa, he gets the impression that the native women must spend hours and hours devising clever new hair-do's. He soon learns, however, that there is no room for originality—each tribe has its own style of hairdressing, and every woman conforms. The women do a great deal of traveling up and down the trails, roads and rivers of Equatorial Africa, visiting friends and relatives. In her hairdress, each woman carries her own identification. The visitor at the Schweitzer Hospital can see, as he walks around the grounds, that dozens of tribes are represented by the feminine patients. The bushy headdresses seen in the photographs above are intermediate stages in the completion of an elaborate tribal hair-do.

One drastic variation of these formalized coiffures comes with the death of a husband. Then a wife may loosen her hairdress, tear off her clothes (except for a loincloth), and roll in the rocky street of the Hospital to express her grief. She will sit and slap her body to drive out Evil Spirits, and the whole family will cry and sing dirges all night every night for a week. The wife will, meanwhile, have cut off all her hair to acknowledge to all who encounter her in the village and elsewhere that she is a widow.

THEY START LIFE BRIGHT, QUICK-WITTED AND CHEERFUL

Four of the most cheerful spirits in the Schweitzer community were these boys, sons of patients, who were kept occupied carrying baskets of leaves and fruit. Like many other youngsters throughout the region, they seem every bit as bright and quick as Western children. They have a ready sense of humor, and pick up the French language, in addition to their own dialect, in early years. The boys asked the American visitors to teach them some English. The boys would grin whenever they saw the foreigners and shout, "Gud moe-ning!"—whatever the hour.

Within a few years they will, in all likelihood, join their elders in the interminable palavers while their wives toil for the family. But it will not be possible to charge this off simply as a lack of industry. It *is* that—but behind it lies an agelong system of values which cannot include the Western world's concept of work. It is inconceivable to them that a Westerner with a wife already "bought" and money saved up will keep on working—and actually enjoy doing it. One native on the staff of a mission was recently sent to Paris for a conference. Upon his return he was asked what impressed him most of all the sights in the fabulous city. His reply: "Can you imagine—I saw men on the streets every morning *hurrying* to get to work!"

THE BOYS GET A FEW YEARS OF SCHOOLING

A few years' schooling in reading, writing (French) and arithmetic is acquired by the boys of the Lambarene district who go to the Protestant mission two miles below the Hospital on the Ogowe River—the same mission that sheltered the Schweitzers when they first arrived in Africa. This congregation gathers each Sunday—the children of the mission school. The service opens with the following Doxology, sung in pure, high-pitched tones by the youths (the vowels being pronounced as in French):

Ñwum'ga Nźamēnya ñga kòm bôr
Ye Yésu eny'a ne Nńyie wā,
Ye Nsisim ô wu vole bie,

Ēsa, Mon ye Mba Mba Nsisim
(Worship God, He who has created man,
And Jesus, He who is our Saviour,
And the Spirit that helps us,
Father, Son and Holy Spirit.)

On this particular Sunday, the native pastor told the story of Cain and Abel, and said, "We do great harm in speaking evil of our brothers. When we hurt our brothers we hurt ourselves. We call forth God's anger against us. God cannot tolerate evil. He drove Cain out of the Garden of Eden. This is death. Jesus has come to bring us peace in the name of God—pardon and life. Let us accept that which He brings us, that 'peace may be with you.'"

YOUNG MAN WITH HIS WORKING CAREER BEHIND HIM

This strapping young man is strong and bright. In the Western world a man of his caliber would be an almost assured success. But in the primitive African milieu there is nothing to acquaint him with—let alone drill him in—the Western habits of industry and of planning for tomorrow and next year. Consequently, work is for women; and—like that of every other man he knows—his career has consisted in working just long enough to accumulate the francs and the produce needed for buying a wife, building a simple hut and a kitchen shelter for her, and clearing and burning a few acres for a plantation.

This young man is a resident of the prosperous fishing village of N'Zoghemitange on a main tributary of the Ogowe above Lambarene. Here, the fish are caught in woven traps set into the river.

When we asked him, "What do you 'do'?" he did not understand. Finally, he shrugged his shoulders and explained that he *has* his wife, and therefore he does not need to work. If he prospers, he will of course expect to acquire another wife, and hope for additional daughters. Meanwhile, he looks a little enviously toward the veritable palace owned by the village chief —a two-story wooden affair, painted blue, with windows of glass.

QUICKLY BUILT—QUICKLY ABANDONED

One of the husband's few duties toward his family is the provision of housing. Native huts are quickly built—and quickly abandoned. As they have been for unknown millennia, the huts are erected in a few days with little labor.

Not just one house but a whole village will often be deserted. Riding on a weekly mail truck over a dirt road through the Equatorial forest, we were puzzled by the number of abandoned villages—the roofs of the houses caved in and the thatched walls hanging in shreds. We asked the native driver about it, and he explained, "All gone to work in town." We mentioned this to a group of old colonials, and they

chuckled good-humoredly at our gullibility.

"Nothing of the kind," one explained. "Several deaths had taken place in a short period, and the rest moved out because they knew the Evil Powers were angry with the whole village."

Visiting a village such as this, one gets a new realization of our dependence upon the generations behind us, each of which left more than it found—more books, more inventions, more discoveries, more universities, more buildings, more factories. Here there is no civilization because nothing extra is produced each generation and passed on to the next.

BAUBLES AND GLITTER—AND PROTEIN-HUNGER

Most promenaders on the waterfront of the town of Lambarene on Big Island look well dressed—but not in the eyes of men like Dr. Schweitzer who know how they live. Many natives have a veritable passion for dressing like the Europeans, and will squander their precious francs on completely worthless but glittering patent-leather dancing pumps, luxury clothing and baubles. Meanwhile, their health suffers from the lack of protein-rich meat and fish—which, if they are working for others, they do not have time to hunt or catch themselves—and the lack of needed articles like blankets. In the towns the height of fashion for the natives is the wearing of European-type sun helmets—although their dark skin does not require such protection.

A large proportion of the promenaders usually seen smoke tobacco. Almost invariably when an *indigène* learns to smoke he becomes an addict. Women especially become strongly habituated, and are often seen with small pipes and cigarettes. Although the natives grow an indigenous tobacco, they scorn it in favor of the more expensive American leaf, or cigarettes. For decades tobacco served as currency, and even missionaries had to carry it—and rum, also—to pay each chief for the privilege of passing his village.

EVERY DAY IS WASHDAY

Many a visitor to Equatorial Africa is surprised to find how much of an effort the *indigènes* make to achieve cleanliness. The above photograph shows one of the most common scenes to be found any day of the week along the riverbanks of the region. Thick bars of crude soap are one of the main items of stock in even the most remote trading post. The *indigènes* scrub their own bodies as thoroughly as they do their clothing. Soon after sunrise each morning, they go down to the river to bathe. They even clean their teeth effectively—with a small piece of charcoal.

The local standards of modesty are observed at least as rigidly as those of the United States or Britain. At our first river-crossing, on the truck trip north from Dolisie to the Ogowe River, we had to cross on a ferry which was driven back and forth by the river current. At either shore it was necessary for one of the crew members to doff his cotton wrap-around and plunge into the water to haul a cable to the landing. Whenever he started to unfasten his lone garment, the women standing on the shore would automatically spin on their heels and stand in this position until they heard him emerge from the water and judged he had had time to cover his person.

FRUIT—AT A STIFF PRICE

Next to hospital buildings, orchards are the most conspicuous features of the Schweitzer community. The Doctor is convinced that greater fruit production and consumption are among Equatorial Africa's most compelling needs. Here, the son of a patient helps harvest the Hospital's grapefruit crop.

In the staff dining hall, heaping bowls of fruit salad—made with oranges, grapefruit, tangerines, and pineapples, in season—are passed at every lunch and dinner. Everyone is encouraged to take several helpings. There was a time, however, when the Hospital staff suffered constantly from a lack of fruit. Through the years precious orchard space was laboriously slashed out of the forest to provide the present plantation. One of the strange minor consequences of World War II was that it made possible the large scale expansion of the Hospital orchards. The war disrupted the private logging operations in the area, and Dr. Schweitzer was able to employ a large crew. Thousands of young fruit trees that the Doctor had raised in a nursery were set out in the newly-cleared land. Dr. Schweitzer admits that building up the Hospital's extensive fruit plantation has cost several years of his life, but considers it eminently worth the price he has had to pay.

•

SIX BANANAS A DAY

Three tons of bananas are being distributed to those patients—the great majority—who are not supplied with their own food. These distributions of rations, at the rate of six average-size bananas a day per person, take place twice a week. The bananas are bought under a contract with an ex-cannibal tribe miles up the Ogowe. After loading their dugout canoes one day, and setting out downriver, the natives arrive at Lambarene in the middle of the next day. The entire operation is supervised by an efficient, administratively skilled chief who sees to it that the men clear the plantations and that their wives plant, cultivate and harvest—all on sched-

ule. The bananas are green because the natives—who obviously have not heard the American radio's admonitions to eat the fruit only when it is yellow and flecked with brown—turn back the ripe ones. They are firmly convinced that ripe bananas cause a wide variety of stomach troubles.

With the point of her bayonet-size knife, the native woman punctures the skin and rips it off around the fruit, instead of the American practice of stripping it lengthwise. The skinned banana is halved and dropped into a small earthen pot or saucepan and boiled. Then it is dipped in palm oil, and eaten.

THE SCHWEITZER HOSPITAL GROWS ITS OWN BUTTER

Palm oil is the natives' butter and cooking fat. Chopping down oil-palm nuts is a task in which one of the patients excels. A heavy machete is used to hack out clumps of the bright orange-red nuts, which crash to the ground. The nuts are removed from the cluster of fiber, in which they grow. Then they are boiled in this kettle, and finally put in a press and crushed. When the semiweekly rations are distributed, a dipperful of this oil is given to each patient. On the Schweitzer plantation, many acres are devoted to the oil palm, which is such an efficient producer of oil that a typical tree will produce approximately three quarts each year.

Palm nuts are subjected to long boiling in the preparation of the oil, and the same is true of the foods which are eaten after being dipped in the oil, namely, bananas and manioc. This prolonged cooking destroys the vitamins, and the indigènes are rendered susceptible to disease. Their vitamin deficiency could be offset by the cultivation and consumption of citrus fruits, and Dr. Schweitzer is carrying on a long range educational program to this end.

Because the natives in the region are becoming less nomadic and more settled, Dr. Schweitzer is hopeful that they can be persuaded to cultivate orchards.

BREAD (MANIOC) LINE FOR PATIENTS

The patients stand in line with their Hospital identification cards and receive their semiweekly rations of bananas and manioc and palm oil (occasionally a bit of fried fish, also, and a little salt). The long broomstick-size objects in the old woman's hand are leaf-wrapped sticks of cooked manioc, the bread of the natives in Equatorial Africa. Westerners eat manioc (or cassava) in the form of the highly refined preparation, tapioca. The native woman digs the roots in her forest plantings, and then soaks them in running water on a riverbank for three to four days—frequently placing them in a half-submerged abandoned dugout. The purpose of this is to leach out the poisons. (Dr. Schweitzer reminds visitors that Stanley lost more than 250 porters on his find-Livingstone expedition when they ate untreated manioc.) The woman cuts the roots into segments, pounds them into a pulp, kneads the pulp with water to form a thick paste, wraps sticks of paste in leaves and finally cooks the sticks in boiling water. At the Hospital each patient is given two sticks a day. The tons of manioc required are purchased from industrious villages that contract to furnish a steady supply to the Hospital. The flavor of the white gummy cooked manioc is, to Westerners, markedly flat.

ACCIDENTAL CONSEQUENCE OF SLAVE TRADE

It is a little-realized fact that Equatorial Africa owes its very living to the cruel slave traders of a century and more ago.

The patients at the Schweitzer Hospital live on the same foods they have at their homes in the forest—bananas, manioc, and palm oil.

Every one of these foods (originally foreign to Africa) that make up the staple diet of the Equatorial African empire was brought in by the slave traders.

The same holds true for the taro root that is used as a substitute for manioc. In addition, oranges, grapefruit, lemons and other fruits that grow so profusely are incidental benefits from the evil slave trade. As Dr. Schweitzer has written, "Equatorial Africa . . . possesses no indigenous fruit trees or fruit bushes. The banana, the yam, cassava (manioc), the sweet potato and the oil palm are not indigenous, but were introduced from the West Indian Islands by the Portuguese." The Portuguese were the principal slavers.

Outside the wards of the Schweitzer Hospital the little fires burn on the ground, a small marmite resting on three stones. There the banana, the manioc, the scrap of meat or fish, the palm oil are mixed to form the usual native dishes. Around the fires the men, women and children squat on the ground, and perform the simple house-

In the forest, a pirogue maker slices off a mouthful of cooked manioc.

In a village near the Hospital, a family gathers around the cook-fire.

A plantation foreman and his wife sit for their evening meal.

A happy chef tests the soup in the Hospital's staff kitchen.

hold duties, and talk and talk and talk. Each little family must seek its own wood in the forest, gather palm nuts, papayas, lemons and mangoes in the plantation.

In a separate building, the meals are prepared for the doctors, nurses and European patients. The cooking is done by a Swiss graduate in dietetics and by a native helper. They employ all their ingenuity to make the indigenous foods palatable for people reared on the foods of the Western world. A typical dinner: ripe papaya fruit as an appetizer, followed by a fish loaf, with taro root (sliced thin and cooked in deep fat) as a potato substitute, and green papaya, boiled, serving as a vegetable dish.

He satisfies his sweet tooth by sucking chunks of sugar cane.

SUMMER PLANTING, WHEN THE RIVER GOES DOWN

In the effort to make the Hospital as nearly self-contained as possible, Dr. Schweitzer has developed one of the largest gardens to be found in the region. It is located on the slope of the river-bank, upstream from the main Hospital buildings.

During the rainy season, much of the garden is deeply flooded, and rank water plants choke the soil. Also, during the wet season, the entire garden tends to slide away. To check this danger, the Doctor has had strong walls built with deep foundations.

One of his uses of the labor made available during World War II was in the con-struction of several hundred yards of these retaining walls. All the stones used had to be transported across the river in the wooden dugouts of the *indigènes*. It was one of the biggest undertakings in the history of the Hospital, and required two dry seasons for its completion.

The garden now measures about fifteen acres, and the successive terraces are filled to a depth of thirty inches with earth that was carried by hand from the ancient compost and garbage dump of a native village formerly located on the top of the hill above the Hospital.

In the garden are grown tomatoes, beans, peas and other vegetables.

First, workmen remove the water plants that grew up while the garden was flooded.

Deep spading is done after the terrace has been uncovered by the falling river.

The surface of the garden is prepared for the planting of seeds and "sets."

Nurse Hedi, who is in charge of the garden, supervises the workmen.

Tomato plants, started in forcing beds, are set out in the garden.

Palm branches are brought from the forest to shade the plants from the hot sun.

"THE TREE WAS DYING"

This is the Doctor's explanation for tearing himself away from urgent duties elsewhere to spend time supervising the replanting and treatment of this tangerine tree. The tree is a living thing, and the Doctor has a sensitive feeling for its health. The tree was planted while the Doctor was away, and the workmen skimped on the size of pit necessary for healthy growth. Dr. Schweitzer requires a pit six feet deep and six feet in diameter for a citrus tree—with the roots to be packed in rich surface soil. This time, he is taking no chances on careless work; he is standing over the two workmen while they widen and deepen the original pit, and repack the roots in rich topsoil.

The Doctor will check the tree's progress every day, and see that it is properly watered.

The Doctor has a great deal of consideration for one fruit that requires no such care as does a citrus tree: the pineapple. He says he finds "a good parable in the pineapple." It grows well—too well at Lambarene—in poor earth. It makes the most of its talents, against difficult odds. As a matter of fact, the pineapple here is a pest. It grows like a weed, and blankets open fields, miles square, with a thick tangle so impenetrable that a man cannot force his way through.

RICE FROM CITRUS ORCHARDS

During his years at Lambarene, the Doctor has planted citrus fruit and harvested rice. One reason he cleared so many acres of the forest and planted citrus trees is that for years he was able to trade the surplus fruit for rice. During the early months of World War II, a surplus of below-standard rice accumulated in the hands of traders who were anxious to unload it, even at drastically reduced prices. Dr. Schweitzer recalls: "A splendid number of sacks was practically forced upon me. Fortunately I had space enough to store it, but the ready money of the Hospital sustained an alarming shrinkage through this purchase. So for three years we lived on this rice, which rendered us great service in feeding our native patients. For in this country a good stock of rice is necessary because, between the harvests, periods always recur when bananas and manioc, which constitute the main diet of the natives, are obtainable in insufficient quantities." As the war progressed, the red tape involved in getting import permits and other papers was so complicated that the Doctor began sending shipments of fruit to villages for free distribution, as a health measure. After the tangerines being carried by this workman and his young helper were harvested, the fruit was shipped to Port Gentil.

RIVER FREIGHT NOW; CROCODILES LATER

Freight for the Schweitzer Hospital and for timber operators on the upper reaches of the Ogowe is transported on this pinasse. The camera has caught Dr. Schweitzer in a characteristic pose—emphasizing his instructions with a gesture. In a few weeks the craft will have to be laid up for the duration of the dry season, for the Ogowe will be a disconnected series of puddles and water holes. Then the crocodiles will come out of hibernation and make life miserable for the *indigènes*. Since this photograph was taken, Dr. Schweitzer has informed the authors that one of his Hospital staff members had stepped on what he thought was a log. It suddenly came to life. "The crocodile bit him cruelly in the leg," reports the Doctor, "tearing out great pieces of flesh. Fortunately, the knee joint was not harmed."

The *indigènes* up and down the Ogowe have several popular nicknames for the Doctor. One is "Mingong" ("Corrugated Iron")—inspired by his introduction of the product for roofs and sidewalls; another is "Misopo" ("Big Abdomen")—a native term of respect reserved for what Americans call Very Important People. The extent of the man's girth has nothing to do with the case! Sometimes the name "Elephant Ear" is applied to him, since he hears everything that is going on.

RIVER TRAVEL DE LUXE

There are two river steamers on the Ogowe which, on alternate weeks, drop mail at Lambarene. This is the "de luxe" steamer, the "Dimbokro," with steam up, ready to start downstream to Port Gentil. The natives, with their goats and chickens, bananas and salt fish, clamber aboard for the twelve-hour trip. (The return voyage, against the current, requires thirty hours when the river is swift.)

The steamers carry export goods to the coast for transshipment. (Tugs, too, are used on the river, for hauling rafts of timber to tidewater.) The Ogowe basin has had a long history of commerce with the outside world, beginning with the nefarious slave trade. The Ogowe watershed was the largest single source of slaves shipped to America. Here one can get the most accurate perspective on the tremendous progress made by the American Negro; for here one can study the very same families whose children, sold to the slavers, were shipped to the Western Hemisphere. The contrast between them and members of these families now in America hits the observer with a shock. One immediately thinks of the celebrated Negro artists, writers, scientists, professional men and women and others who have added so much to the depth and variety of American culture.

TRADER HORN'S COMPANY

The oldest trading post (or "factory") in the region is that of Hatton & Cookson, the firm represented by Trader Horn, who came to the district in 1874 (two years before the American mission). The present factory is located on Big Island, in the village of Lambarene; but in Trader Horn's time the concern's property was located at Adolinanongo, on the shelf of land immediately above the present Schweitzer Hospital.

For decades, many of the big trading companies operated in a manner that coupled a certain degree of paternalism with their profit-making activities. For example, these companies refused to sell liquor to the *indigènes,* and liquor consumption was limited to a considerable extent by the fact that the native palm wine required a great deal of labor to make and would keep only a few days. This meant that liquor was drunk mainly on feast days. Nowadays, a substantial proportion of the cash income of the average *indigène* is spent for imported spirits.

In front of the building above, Mohammedan traders from northern regions set up their tables and sell cigarettes (either single cigarettes or full packages), matches, soap, buttons, thread, needles and other trifles.

HOUSING DE LUXE

One of the finest examples of native housing adapted for Western-style living is this home of a French timber exploiter. The walls are of thin poles, with a wide opening below the roof for free circulation of air. The hot air rises into the high-pitched roof (right) and escapes through ports. The rooms inside are spacious. Cooking is done in the little house adjoining (also a native practice).

The timberman and his wife offset their isolation by subscribing to European and American journals, which arrive at Lambarene on the weekly mail boat and are carried overland by one of the owner's American-built logging trucks.

IN THE LITTLE FOREST

The Schweitzer Hospital is located in what is called the Little Forest. Here, the trees do not grow so big as in the Great Forest farther inland. The two types of forest, however, are equally dense, and the Little Forest has considerable marketable timber in it. The above photograph shows the thick mat of ferns and vines that blankets the forest floor, beneath the tangle of interlocked tree branches.

The two axmen shown on the opposite page are felling an okoume that is about 150 years old and stands 120 feet high. The salmon-colored okoume wood is exported to Europe and North America. The natives use the okoume for dugout canoes; the whites, for a finishing surface on plywood. This tree contains some ten tons of merchantable wood. This tree trunk will be allowed to lie on the ground for two months, drying out, before it is "bucked" into short logs for transport. A friend of Dr. Schweitzer, André Thalmann, a timber exploiter, is seen standing beside a squared-off mahogany log. Mahogany, incidentally, is used as a common building material here, and even as firewood. It is valued far below forest products such as paddock and rosewood, cherished for pianos and fine cabinet work (although in former decades these woods, too, were valued by operators of river steamers in

Equatorial Africa as prime fuels for stoking their boilers).

Thousands of natives in Equatorial Africa get cash (for buying wives, among other things) by working in the timber.

Logging accidents send a certain proportion of the workmen to the Schweitzer Hospital, although the safety record is considered to be quite high.

Occasionally a workman is brought in for treatment of snakebite. (Even though the familiar allegorical drawings showing the African jungle as a tangle of serpents are somewhat exaggerated, snakes are a constant danger.)

MANY NATIVE CRAFTS STILL PRESERVED

Above: The ropemaker above produces almost all the cord required in the Schweitzer Hospital community. The fibers of pineapple leaves, when stripped and twisted together, make some of the strongest rope in the world. Dr. Schweitzer tells of the ocean liner that tore loose from its moorings in a storm and wrecked a dock in a European port. "It should have been tied with our Lambarene pineapple-rope," he laughs.

Below: This maker of basket-weave fish traps is proud of the durability of his handiwork—which will last for years of hard usage.

Above: Sturdy clothes are made on the Hospital premises at low cost for the use of the native staff. Heavy blue denim is sewn into overalls, trousers and work aprons. The workman here is operating a hand-cranked sewing machine. He does not feel this is women's work, because the operation of anything so complicated as a sewing machine is reserved for the men in many areas of Equatorial Africa. In larger towns crews of men with sewing machines are seen converting cloth into garments and repairing old clothing.

Below: At the Schweitzer Hospital, women are permitted to sew by machine.

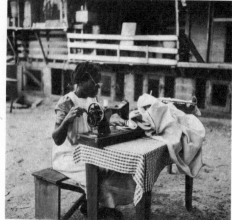

Above: This is the way green-leaf roof tiles are made by the natives of Equatorial Africa. This young wife, in the village of N'Zoghemitanga on the N'Goungie River, bends the long leaves, which grow on the edges of swamps, over the two parallel sticks, and then stitches them to the framework with dry reeds. Dr. Schweitzer had so much difficulty in getting roof tiles from the natives in the first years of the Hospital that he switched to corrugated iron, pioneering in its use in the region.

Below: The fluffed-up kapok fiber is stuffed into mattresses and pillows for use in the Hospital community.

Above: A woman in the same village works reeds from a nearby swamp into a mat. This village has one of the highest standards of living in the region, and perhaps this prosperity stems in part from the vigorous preservation of the old crafts.

Below: Mattress-making is one of the arts developed at the Schweitzer Hospital. First nuts are harvested from the kapok trees found in the district. These trees have trunks that are enormously thick at the base and taper to a thin peak. Then the fluffy white fiber that surrounds the nuts is removed. Workmen then tear the fibers apart, and painstakingly remove impurities.

EMPLOYEE NO. 1

Basile A'Atombogogno, the Hospital's shoemaker, was Dr. Schweitzer's first employee in 1913. He has worked as a carpenter, medical assistant, fruit picker and general helper. Here he is photographed the day before his seventieth birthday.

He is the only person in the region who remembers General de Brazza.

On the next day, a Sunday, Basile and his wife dressed in their best bib and tucker (right) and posed for a formal portrait with his wife's sister and her daughter. The European staff, led by Dr. Schweitzer bearing a cake, marched to Basile's cottage, and everyone presented his congratulations.

ANOTHER HALF-DAY GONE

The pump has broken down again. Laboriously, Dr. Schweitzer has to take it down, find the broken part and repair it, with the assistance of the tinsmith. Then he reassembles it, and now the first flow of water comes—four hours later. The precious pump is the Doctor's personal responsibility. Even though it keeps breaking down, he wishes the *indigènes* would use it more. Too many of them dip up polluted water from the river rather than walk a few more yards to the pump.

"The other day," he comments, "I saw a native woman jerking the pump handle sideways, instead of up and down. I asked her what she was doing. She did not know. She did not even know what it was. I am sure her jerkings did not help it!

"Almost every two weeks I have to repair it. Nobody else can do it. Sometimes it takes all day.

"We have to simplify everything here, for the natives cannot run the machinery and take care of it. I have to do it myself. We have no electric plant for that reason. Besides, if we break anything, it is very difficult to get the new parts. I write off for them and they reply, 'Yes, we will send them to you in six months.'"

Recently the Doctor has received a shipment of pipe and has brought water under pressure to the staff compound.

PREACHER OF THE GOSPEL

Of dignified bearing is this native pastor, visiting the Schweitzer Hospital for a minor operation.

European and American missionaries in the region look forward to the day when all Christian schools, churches and missions can be turned over to *indigènes* like him.

Religion is a subject of great gravity at Lambarene, but occasionally there is a bit of humor connected with it. For example, one day the Doctor was asked by the administration to furnish a list of all the natives, Hospital staff and others, who lived in the Doctor's Village. It was necessary to indicate in each case the race and religion. The foreman in charge of the plantation workmen was asked to prepare the list and submit it to the Doctor. When the latter looked it over he was surprised to find under the rubric of "religion" in a good many cases the word "freethinker."

"What does this mean?" he asked the foreman.

"The freethinkers are those who are neither Catholic nor Protestant," was the reply.

"But those people are pagans," the Doctor said.

"That's true," said the foreman, "but I thought it sounded better to say 'freethinker.'"

"MISSION CATHOLIQUE!"

This identification is called out by Dr. Schweitzer to those in his pirogue as he passes these buildings on Big Island. Although a Protestant clergyman, Dr. Schweitzer has always had friendly relations with the nearby Roman Catholics. He remembers the time when, during the First World War, he and other non-French prisoners of war were transferred to Europe for internment. The Father Superior of the Catholic mission was prominent in the delegation that went to the village to see the Schweitzers off.

At this mission occurred, a few years ago, a case of mass poisoning. The mission's staff had been warned by the students that bad medicine was being prepared in the village supplying eggs for the kitchen. The whites scoffed until they fell violently ill during supper a few days later. A pirogue was dispatched immediately for Dr. Schweitzer; he was able to use a stomach pump before the results were fatal—although one woman teacher was close to death for days. Later it was discovered the rumor had been circulated that the school was forcing one of its girl students from the "egg" village to go to Europe with a white man. Actually, the girl was preparing to run off with the man and had fabricated the story in order to make herself appear innocent at home.

The great, wide, wonderful world is faced by this bright-eyed youngster.

This elderly patient suddenly turned and found himself staring into the camera.

A teen-ager with a mandolin in a village several miles up the Ogowe.

A seller of betel nuts smiles as if business among the patients were good.

Given new glasses, this Moslem reads the Koran for the first time in years.

A teen-ager and his younger brother wait for their father to be diagnosed.

He came for a minor complaint and learned that he has leprosy.

The photographer, looking for an *indigène* Madonna and child, found these.

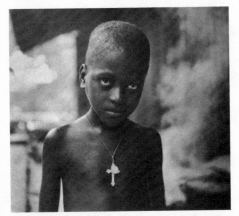

The cross and the medal mean that this lad attends a mission school.

This short-statured workman supervises the Hospital laundry.

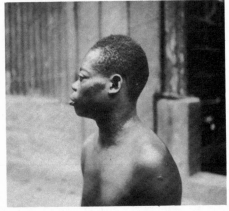

A swelling of the neck brought him to the Hospital.

This handsome Galoa came to the Hospital from a downriver village.

WORK IN PROGRESS

Late at night, under the flickering light of a kerosene lamp, the Doctor labors at the writing table in his tiny study-office-bedroom. He expresses deep anxiety about completing the third volume of *The Philosophy of Civilization*. As he finishes chapters, he piles them on the top shelf above his head. Chapters on which he is still working are hung by strings—"the way a hunter hangs up his pheasants!" he laughs—to nails behind him. At his left elbow is an advance copy of *Albert Schweitzer: An Anthology* [*] which the authors took to Africa.

In his first interview [**] on world affairs in more than a decade, Dr. Schweitzer told us: "We must substitute the power of understanding the truth that is really true for propaganda; a noble kind of patriotism which aims at ends that are worthy of the whole of mankind, for the patriotism current today; a humanity with a common civilization, for idolized nationalisms; a restored faith in the civilized state, for a society which lacks true idealism . . . a faith in the possibility of progress, for a mentality stripped of all true spirituality. These are our tasks."

---

[*] Beacon Press, Boston, and Harper & Brothers, New York; edited by Charles R. Joy.

[**] *The Christian Register* CXXVI (1947), September, page 320.

"The Old Doctor"

The room in which Dr. Schweitzer works at Günsbach, where these lines are written, is a plain and simple study-bedroom. Nowhere is there the slightest sign of luxury. In the corner stands a white iron bed, like a *lit de camp*. Beside it is a small wooden table on which lie a few pieces of paper and the stub of a pencil, so that even in the middle of the night the Doctor can switch on the light and jot down any vagrant thoughts that come to him. Over his head on a shelf is the fine model of an eighteenth-century sailing ship given to him by friends in Holland. Underneath the shelf is a picture of a negro in the Bartholdi statuary group at Colmar erected in honor of the French Admiral Bruat. The negro's noble face, symbolizing the African continent, made a profound impression upon the young Albert Schweitzer. (The Second World War destroyed the monument, but fortunately the fine head of the negro was saved.) On the right wall beside the bed is a sketch of St. Thomas, where Johann Sebastian Bach was cantor; a water color of St. Nicholas at Strassburg, where Schweitzer preached so often; another of the River Ogowe painted from the Doctor's room at Lambarene.

A plain, unfinished wooden table with two drawers is the Doctor's only desk. As he sits there writing he can lift up his eyes to the wall before him and see faces that are dear to him: the strong, bearded face of his pastor father; his mother's face, friendly, affectionate; his favorite elder sister, now dead; the picture of another sister; the lovely head of his daughter, Rhena. There is a water color of the old town of Kaysersberg where he was born; another of the railway station at Günsbach; an etching of the neighboring meadows with the tall church spire—destroyed during the recent war—rising in the midst of the clustering buildings. Behind him is a cupboard for his clothes, and a very narrow bookcase of eight shelves, eighteen inches wide, where a few books stand. In the corner is another wooden table on which some books of music rest, and some characteristic records of sermons preached in St. Nicholas, tied together as always with string. There are three plain chairs, the floor is bare, the walls are white. The room is just as he left it when he hastily returned to Africa before the Second World War. The calendar still reads, "February, 1939."

Here in this room Dr. Schweitzer has worked on such books as *The Indian Religions and Their Development,* and his monumental work *The Philosophy of Civilization,* the first volume of which had been prepared in his father's parsonage at Günsbach from 1919 to 1923. The simplicity and plainness of this room reflect the character of the man. There are rooms in the house that are larger, sunnier, rooms with beautiful prospects over meadows and mountains. This room with its window opening on the street is the one he has selected for his bedroom and study. Here simplicity takes on the nature of greatness.

The Doctor's room in Lambarene is much the same. There, too, is a plain, unvarnished table, an exact duplicate of the Günsbach table, which he made for himself.

"Look," he said to me once, "this is the desk I have used for many years. The termites have eaten part of it." He showed me the long tunnels made in the wood. "But I like it." At that Lambarene table he had made the first draft of his famous memorial address on the one hundredth anniversary of Goethe's death. There he had written *Out of My Life and Thought.* So, whether written in Europe or Africa, his books have come, not out of pampered ease and comfort, but truly out of his life and thought. Living by preference a life devoid of all luxury he has sought instinctively for that reality that lies behind the tapestries and underneath the cushions of modern life.

Not that his existence has been in any way a hard, monastic life of rigid self-discipline, nor even a cloistered life of seclusion. His study-bedroom at Lambarene is cluttered with workmen's tools, and from it he directs the manifold activities of the Hospital. His study-bedroom at Günsbach looks out on the road to Münster; from it he can watch the men and women pass, and chat with them at times. To them he is simply "Monsieur Albert," except when they talk to the visitor about their Docteur Schweitzer. They see him sitting on the front steps of his house, climbing the hill to his own Kanzenrain to enjoy the lovely view over the peaceful valley, or taking his evening walk toward Münster and resting on his bench by the side of the road for a few minutes before turning homeward again. He is one of them, a simple villager in his native land, a "pine tree of the Vosges."

So to the world at large he is also the same plain, simple, unpretending, genuine person. He described his meeting with Dr. Wilfred Thomason Grenfell in Edinburgh as that of "the hippopotamus and the polar bear." When he was lecturing in Scotland, the presiding officer before the meeting turned to Dr. Schweitzer and asked him how he wished to be introduced. "Oh," said Dr. Schweitzer, "tell them that this fellow on the platform that looks like a shaggy dog is Albert Schweitzer."

This is indeed the man, unassuming and sincere, who moves about among his fellow men as one of them, who serves them with no sense of sacrifice, but as one who finds the fulfillment of his life in the path of service. And as he walks along his way, he hardly knows how much healing there is in his shadow.

Years ago a visitor inquired into the secret of his amazing accomplishments. "You are still a comparatively young man and you have written books of considerable importance. How have you been able to do so much?"

Dr. Schweitzer's eyes began to gleam. "I don't dare to tell you," he replied.

"Please tell me," the stranger urged. "I will treat anything you say with complete confidence."

"All right," said the doctor, "I'll tell you. I don't go in for sports." And he burst into laughter.

Dr. Schweitzer's life is a pruned life, which bears a rich and luscious fruit because its strength is not sapped by extraneous activities. He has planned his life carefully, he has selected the ends to be served with wisdom and vision, and then he has permitted nothing else to distract his attention. Only so has he been able to achieve distinction in philosophy, theology, music and medicine.

This is one reason why he does not waste time on superfluous things. He has only one necktie at Lambarene. "Why have more? You can't wear more than one at a time." I went with him to pay an official call upon the district administrator.

"Bring a necktie and a coat," he told me. So we were paddled across the river to the little town, and climbed the hill to the administrative center.

"Now," said he, as we approached the house, "I must put on my tie." He pulled a little bow tie out of his pocket, buttoned up the collar of his shirt and put on the tie. "This is the only tie I have owned since 1928," he said with a grin, "and I haven't had it on for five months."

A few minutes later he put on his white coat, but I noticed that he was still wearing his old, darned khaki trousers. A half-hour later when we emerged from the office of the administrator the first thing he did was to pull off his bowtie, with a sigh of relief. He was his old, natural, simple self again.

Once after spending an evening hour in my room he left his hat behind him. The next morning I returned it to him.

"Ah," he said with a sigh of relief, "you are an honest man. When I mislay my hat I am terrified for fear I have lost it. That hat is an old friend of mine. My friends in Europe have often offered to buy me a new hat, but I always refuse. When I go home I buy a new hatband and a new ribbon, and then my hat is as good as new.

"When I was a young man of eighteen I had at Günsbach an old tan coat. Later when I used to return to Günsbach on vacation I always hunted up this coat immediately (it was kept in my closet for me) and wore it all the time I was at home. If my mother knew I was coming she always put it on a chair in front of my table, so that I should not have to look for it when I arrived. But

TAKING NO CHANCES WITH SUNSTROKE

From sunrise to sundown, every minute the Doctor is out of doors he has a sun helmet clamped firmly on his head. When he first went to Africa he learned of the peril to a white man of even a few seconds' exposure of the head to the tropical sun. There have been so many cases of sunstroke, with fatalities, in Equatorial Africa that the Doctor takes no chances himself and sternly shouts, "Casque! Casque!" to any white person who is careless. On this voyage, the sun was behind the Doctor, and he protected the back of his neck with his jacket. There were two white sun-umbrellas, but of course the Doctor insisted that the visitors use them. (Because of being constantly covered, the white person living on the equator is likely to remain untanned and even pale. The fashionable tan of Florida and the Riviera is completely unknown.)

The Doctor sat himself down on a plain wooden box in his dugout canoe and motioned his visitors to comfortable canvas chairs. When they protested he said, "No argument! This is not a congress or a parliament!" To speed the paddling, he called out, "Hurry up! The American visitors like to go fast!" Even though they know there will be such pressure, the workmen argue among themselves for the privilege of going a-voyaging.

DISTRICT HEADQUARTERS

On the porch of the Lambarene District administration building the Doctor signs the vital records—births and deaths that have taken place at the Hospital. This is the first time he has taken time off to visit the headquarters in five months, and he has a stack of records to cope with.

The tides of war—Free France vs. Vichy—swirled over this hill, which overlooks the town of Lambarene and the broad Ogowe, and Dr. Schweitzer recalls those dreaded days of 1940, and also the tremendous sense of relief that came on V-E Day in 1945. Late that evening he wrote, "I fetched from its shelf the little book with the sayings of Lao-tse and read his impressive words on war and victory: 'Weapons are disastrous implements, no tools for a noble being. Only when he can do no otherwise, does he make use of them . . . Quiet and peace are for him the highest. He conquers but he knows no joy in this. He who would rejoice in victory, would be rejoicing in murder. . . . At the victory celebration, the general should take his place as is the custom at the funeral ceremonies. The slaughter of human beings in great numbers should be lamented with tears of compassion. Therefore should he who has conquered in battle bear himself as if he were at a festival of mourning.'"

when I came back from my first stay in Africa, it was no longer there. My youngest sister, who had always scolded me for my attachment to this old coat—whose tan color had taken on with the years a greenish tone—had got rid of it by giving it to a beggar. I was very sad about it, for when I used to put on that coat I seemed to be carried back through the years to the happy days of my student life. I would much rather she had given the beggar the finest coat I had."

Dr. Schweitzer has only one child of his own, and he has been separated from her for many years because of his long African sojourns. He has never seen his four grandchildren, the oldest of whom is eight. But he is very fond of children. While I was at the Hospital, the little daughter of a white woman awaiting her confinement ate regularly with us. She sat with her mother at the far end of the table, away from the door. Dr. Schweitzer would come in, hang up his sun helmet, walk down the room and bow profoundly to Collette, make some pleasant remark on her hair ribbon, her hair-do or her dress, and ask about her health. Collette would respond just as seriously. He was to her just another child, which is the highest compliment a child can pay to an adult. The Hospital always has small children in it, new born babies, motherless children, children of the patients of the Hospital staff. Many duties press hard upon the Doctor, but there is nothing he loves better than to chat and romp with the children.

Nowhere else, however, is the distinctive quality of his spirit so clearly revealed as it is in his treatment of animals. The natives in the vicinity all know that if they bring to him a hurt animal or one that has been left motherless, they will be well rewarded. And so the yard among the buildings occupied by the white staff is always thronged with animals.

The weaverbirds build their nests in his beloved palm trees by the house, kill the trees by stripping all the fiber from the leaves to make their nests, eat the grain spread out for the hens, but nobody dares disturb them. Geese, hens, turkeys and ducks, African sheep and goats wander about at will. Monkeys roam about the verandas; dogs and cats are everywhere. In the branches high overhead a little white owl gazes with fixed eyes upon a platter of fish held out to lure him, but does not dare descend while people stand around. He sleeps under the veranda roof at night, however, and Dr. Schweitzer feeds him little pieces of meat. Under the house are the poultry and the antelopes. While the latter are small they are put in a pen in the house beside Dr. Schweitzer's study, and in the evening they are loosed to roam about. When they get bigger they are banished to pens beneath the house, where Dr. Schweitzer goes to feed them with slices of peeled oranges. The latest addition to the Doctor's family is Pamela, a miniature antelope very intelligent and graceful, who will never be higher than twelve inches. In the courtyard parrots fly about the trees, but they too have their perch inside the dining room to which they are brought for their meals.

Whenever the Doctor crosses the courtyard a half-dozen dogs come to greet him. He stops to talk with them. Tchu-tchu is the favorite among them. It is amusing to watch her. All the dogs follow the Doctor to the foot of the steps that lead to the dining room. There all the dogs stop, except Tchu-tchu. She precedes the Doctor up the stairs into the dining room, where she takes her place behind the Doctor's chair. He never forgets to toss her some scraps from the table even before he seats himself.

In the dispensary of the Hospital, Sisi, the cat, has a similar place of privilege. Whenever the Doctor sits at his table there, Sisi jumps on the table to demand attention. Sisi's mother was still nursing the kitten when she was stolen by some natives who were leaving the Hospital. The Doctor saved the kitten's life by feeding it with a medicine dropper. Often the Doctor works in the dispensary in the evening, writing notes to accompany his prescriptions. On such occasions Sisi lies down, puts her head on the Doctor's left arm and goes to sleep. From that time on he works with one hand, for Sisi must not be disturbed. Often the Doctor's arm is asleep before Sisi wakes up.

Yet there is wisdom in his relations with animals. I was patting one of the dogs one afternoon, when the Doctor cautioned me not to do that.

"The dogs are likely to be very dirty," he said. "They roll around on the ground and they may have the germs of dysentery in their hair. It is really not safe to touch them here at the Hospital."

His love for animals extends far. In my room one afternoon he quietly arose without saying a word, picked up a glass from the table and a blotter from the desk, went to the screen and caught a bee, which he took to the door and released in the open air. Then, still without a word, he resumed his conversation.

I was sitting beside him on a wall one day, and noticed an ant on his collar. I started to brush it away, but he quickly protested. "No, no, leave it alone. It's my ant," he said.

I was walking across a level field at the Catholic mission with him another day. In the old days a native village stood there. We came across a patch of burned grass.

"I never burn a field," he said. "Think of all the insects that perish in such a fire! Already in the popular Chinese treatise, *Kan Ying Pien* (Book of Rewards and Punishments), which is as venerable for its exalted thought as for its age, it is forbidden to set fire to the fields for the purpose of the hunt. 'If one sets fire to the fields in hunting,' we read there in explanation of this command, 'he not only causes the death of animals, but of insects also. . . . If we cause them to perish, we rebel against Heaven, by destroying a multitude of its creatures. This is the greatest of crimes.' As I read the words of this venerable book, where pity for all living things is recognized for the first time as a human duty,

AN ARRIVAL AND A DEPARTURE

The Doctor arrives at the government post downriver to pay an official call on the Chief of the Lambarene District, Nelson Lamothe, an old colonial. When asked what the Hospital means to the natives of the region, the Chief replied, "It means everything! It is indispensable. It is a kind of salvation for them. But, alas, they don't know it! Except for consideration within an immediate family or tribe, the natives know nothing of the kind of disinterested, unselfish generosity that Dr. Schweitzer represents. For example, the native medicine men use their medicines, but not for reasons of devotion to the health of their fellows. Rather, they use their drugs to build up power in the village. They will give mild poisons to people and then cure them in order to gain control over them." *Right:* Usually after two years' service in the oppressive Equatorial African climate, staff members must get a long rest in the outside world before continuing their labors in the Hospital. Most staff members do lecturing while on leave, and raise money for the work of the Hospital. Today, Dr. and Mrs. Ladislas Goldschmid and their son leave in a government motorboat —the doctor also helps operate on a part-time basis an official provincial hospital for sleeping sickness—for Port Gentil, where they will take a steamer for France.

SHOPPING IN A TRADING POST

The natives and Europeans go to "factories" to buy their supplies. This trading post lies below the hill on which stands the local government headquarters. The Doctor buys a gross of screws for carpentry work at the Hospital. (He decides not to buy the aluminum roaster he is inspecting.) A larger "factory" stocks a variety of merchandise that has to be seen to be believed. Here, for the use of both natives and Europeans, are shelves of:

Canned foods: tinned dried green peas, chicken soup, carrots, cabbage, sauerkraut, sardines, *pâté de foie gras.*

Liquor: wines and brandies of all kinds, from cheap *vin ordinaire* to Chablis.

Cosmetics: Schiaparelli perfume; Gemey, Roger & Gallet perfumes; lipsticks.

Clothing: shirts, suit coats, vests—both new and second-hand (used articles of clothing are shipped into Equatorial Africa at the rate of several millions a year).

Hardware: knives, screwdrivers, saws, planes, hammers, pliers, pans, kettles.

Miscellaneous: cigarettes, table games, Chinese puzzles, vegetable seeds.

This particular factory does not stock shoes but others do; and Dr. Schweitzer tells of the patent leather dancing pumps purchased by one of his early staff.

I think of the days towards the end of dry season here in this country, when the natives burn vast areas of brush and forest, to make room for their plantations. Night after night I see the light of these great conflagrations all around the horizon, and my heart is filled with pity."

To care for all the animals about him seems to be second nature for Dr. Schweitzer. Whenever he has a small fawn in the pen beside his study, he keeps a rug spread over the pedals of his piano, lest the little animal break its legs among them. He once had a small porcupine in his room; one evening when he was playing the piano, he glanced behind him, and was thrilled to see the little animal dancing on the floor in time with the music.

His attitude toward the natives is also dictated by both pity and comprehension. But a certain firmness is associated with his kindness. He demands obedience of them.

Many times I had occasion to witness what the Doctor calls smilingly his moral imperialism. This is based upon his long experience, and it is softened by his natural kindness and by his comprehension.

When the natives receive an order from him, he permits them to make any comments upon it which seem good to them. If these comments seem well founded, he considers them and acts upon them. But, if he sticks to his original decision, he does not permit them to bring up the matter again.

If he has wronged a native he is quick to admit it and to make amends when there is an opportunity. A woman came to the Hospital one day with a sick daughter who had to have a great deal of care and medicine. In return for this and for the food that both of them received daily she had to work in the garden several hours a day pulling up weeds. This she did with very bad grace and with great indolence. One day the Doctor came to the garden and noticed that she had done practically nothing for several days. He scolded her for it very vehemently and went away leaving her ashamed and disconsolate. A little while afterward, leaving for a moment his work in the Hospital, he returned to the garden, spoke to her with great gentleness and gave her a little present to console her. In spite of everything he had not been able to bear the thought of having hurt the woman.

In relation to the white staff I noticed the same mixture of firmness, understanding and kindness. He permits them to state freely their objections to any measures taken or orders given, and in the light of their comments often changes his decisions. But whenever he stands by his opinion he expects the staff to conform and to trust in him. He requests of new arrivals that they wait until they have gained some experience before they begin to criticize. He seeks advice, however, from all the doctors and nurses who have been with him for a long time, and in certain cases lets them act in accordance with their own judgment, even when it differs from his own.

A number of times at the Hospital I heard people say, "The old Doctor has still the strength to work, but not the strength to argue." I have an idea that he himself put these words into circulation.

Few men in the world have a mind so richly stocked with general information and so excellent a memory. There is no intellectual conceit about him, just a quiet confidence in the physical, mental and spiritual equipment with which he has been endowed. It is the content that counts, not the form of it.

There has been nothing formal or academic about his life, in spite of his university associations and his many books. "My life has unfolded like a romance," he once said. It has, indeed, been a romance to him, full of fascinating experiences, ever changing, ever new, and the central theme of it has been love. He has been in love with life, with his work, with the people around him. "People call me a man of action," he wrote, "but they do not understand me. I am really a dreamer." Even his friends sometimes fail to realize how much of a dreamer he is. They hear his hearty, boisterous laugh. They listen to his stimulating talk. They see the light play brilliantly upon the many facets of his brain. They see his life pouring out in vigorous activity, in tireless service for others. Yet he is quite truthful when he says, "I am by nature very uncommunicative concerning my private life. It is a trait that I got from my mother."

His music is a part of the romance of his life, and in his music, at least, he is communicative. Songs without words sometimes reveal more of a man's soul than lengthy ballads. Schweitzer is most himself when he sits on an organ console or on a piano bench. "I have a passion for music," he says. "It is like another man's passion for wine or tobacco."

Something deep within him finds expression also in his wonder at the glory of nature. It is not the formal and artificial in nature that appeal to him. Formal parks displease him. Flower gardens hold no interest for him. Cut flowers are a violation of the sanctity of life. But fruit trees thrill him. They fulfill their destiny and they delight the heart of man and beast. We were walking along in the orchard one afternoon, when suddenly he stopped and said, "You are going to eat some strawberries. Have you a knife?" I gave him my penknife. He stooped down, and picked a little round fruit, which he cut in two. Taking out the center of it he gave it to me, and then cut another fruit for a companion who was with me. For some minutes he fed us ripe guavas. They were, indeed, delicious, like sweet strawberries. We greatly enjoyed them—but his delight, I believe, was even greater than ours.

As we walked about the Hospital grounds he was constantly stopping to nudge me and to point out something interesting or beautiful: a long line of African sheep returning from their daily foraging, with three of his ducks bringing up the end of the procession; the pelican swooping in to its perch; the weaverbirds eating the grain spread out for his hens; the spreading shade of the mangos; the glorious crowns of the palm trees. I have sat with him many times in the late afternoon on a low wall, while the antelopes played around us, and his eyes grew soft as he looked down through the trees to the river. "How lovely it is!" he would say over and over again.

All this he has made his own. The loveliness around him is now a part of his life. Indeed much of it is his life, for the Doctor's village and the Doctor's plantation are but projections of his indomitable spirit. All this that he sees is his own past written in wood and stone, in orchard and garden.

When Dr. Schweitzer decided to go out to Africa to minister to the natives he believed he would have to sacrifice his music, his writing and his financial independence. He no longer talks about sacrifice except in very petty matters. The sacrifices he makes no one knows much about: leaving his desk to get some nails or to see that the pirogues are in the water, leaving the Hospital to watch the natives put up a fence to keep the geese out of his garden. These, indeed, are sacrifices, but it is no sacrifice to live and work at Lambarene. It is to him a blessed privilege.

One sacrifice, however, he may be called upon to make increasingly in the years that remain, a sacrifice that will be hard indeed. More and more the eyes of men are fixed upon him. More and more his privacy is being invaded. The world is becoming interested in his thought, but even more it is becoming interested in the man himself. From the glare of publicity he shrinks as he never shrinks from the most exhausting labor. Excessive adulation brings agony to his soul. Unrestrained praise is like a stinging lash to his spirit. If the simplicity and naturalness with which he has surrounded himself all his life should be torn away it would leave him naked in an icy blast. So the question we raise is this: Can his searching philosophy of life be brought to bear upon the ailing modern world, without wrecking his own happiness? Will the world be gentle to him?

He knows, of course, that he must suffer the consequences of his work. In this world where we live it is impossible that the philosophy of reverence for life should win support without attracting attention to its author. For us today a man's personality is much more closely tied to his ideas and his work than it was in preceding generations. This is not a sign of idle curiosity. We wish to understand a personality, its nature, its worth, that we may perceive the spiritual forces that emanate from it and give authority to the ideals it professes. Dr. Schweitzer must understand that even his personal life no longer belongs entirely to himself. We who are his friends know how much all this costs him. But we are also sure that he will find a way of remaining himself, of protecting his simplicity and naturalness even though the eyes of men are fixed upon him.

NEW BURDEN

The Doctor hurries down the steps of the post office in the town of Lambarene. In his hands is a burden—the burden of late hours spent in writing replies by hand. Most of his correspondence must be done in the midnight hours, in the flickering, yellowish light cast by a kerosene lamp. There, he strains his eyes and gets painful writer's cramp. He insists on writing, himself, letters to relatives of persons whose lives the Hospital has not been able to save, and many other letters that are required in the operation of a busy hospital. At the same time, he carries on a heavy correspondence with friends and supporters of the Hospital overseas.

The Doctor said he wanted to show his visitors the spot where he was standing once, the previous winter, when he started through a packet of mail; from the top letter he learned that emergency needs had caused a drastic reduction in the Hospital's bank balance, and from the bottom letter he learned that a deposit had been received from the United States more than sufficient to cover the drain. The Lambarene institution carries on in its entirety on the dollars and francs and pounds and kroner mailed by friends and admirers of the Doctor and the Hospital, living in every part of the Western world.

BEGINNING OF THE DAY

Left: At six-thirty every morning, and at two every afternoon, the native non-medical workmen at the Hospital community gather at the steps below the Doctor's tiny office-study-bedroom. They are checked off on their records by one of the nurses, and given their assignments—to perform the endless tasks involved in operating a nearly self-contained community of some three hundred persons. When the workmen are sent off on their assignments, a nurse or other staff member always goes along to serve as a foreman. The present authors went into the orchard one afternoon to help two *indigènes* pick oranges, which were becoming overripe.

The nurse who was with us was called back to the Hospital. Within three minutes one of the workmen had disappeared, and the other one was found nonchalantly paddling a dugout in circles on a nearby stream. Native foremen cannot be used because they dare not chastise another for fear of having a spell cast on them.

Right: The work of the Hospital, with its forty buildings and its 220 acres of land, is never done. Here, workmen during the dry months repair the paths damaged during the long rainy seasons. The paths are raised slightly to provide drainage. A traction surface is applied in the form of palm-nut shells rolled into the earth.

From the Rising of the Sun

Darkness lies over the tall trees of the forest. The okoumes, the great kapok trees, the graceful palm trees are hidden in the blackness of the night. No native treads the hidden jungle trails, which belong now to the panther, the gorilla, the wild boar. But the night is alive with sound, the cries of beasts who hunt and are hunted, the rustle of the wind in the banana trees, the whistle of parrots and their soft cuckoo, the chatter of monkeys, the ceaseless shrill of the crickets. The jungle becomes vocal, for the night is coming to an end.

There is a stirring that precedes the dawn. A rooster crows, and another in the distance replies. From the tops of the palm trees the weaverbirds take their heads from under their black and yellow wings, and begin to talk to one another in a squeaky chatter. Africa has many birds without song and many flowers without perfume. The eastern skies grow pale with soft hues of gray and rose, and the nests of the weaverbirds begin to show against the sky, a hundred dark balls hanging from the spreading fronds. Beneath the house the antelopes begin to move, the pelican that roosts beside the Doctor's door stretches his wings, preens his feathers, and looks about him. A spread of wide pinions and he is off to the river for his breakfast of fish.

The little community of sick and well awakes. The African day comes quickly on, as the sun rises steeply from the horizon. This is the equator. Mists lie on the river. The light begins to reveal the chrome yellow of ripening grapefruit, the bronze of oranges, the gold of lemons and the dark green clumps of breadfruit under large-fingered leaves.

From the island across the branch of the Ogowe comes, soft and beautiful, mellowed by the distance, the sound of bells from the Catholic mission. It is six o'clock.

Blue wisps of smoke begin to rise from the red roofs of the native quarters. Down by the river the men and women are washing their clothes, their babies, themselves. Pails of water are filled, then carried off on black curly heads. Over the little wood fires before the huts the green pig-bananas and the manioc are being boiled.

Half past six. The clang of the first gong comes repeatedly from behind the dining hall. The natives call it the Doctor's voice, and the workmen assemble in their ragged shorts and bubus. Their legs and their feet are bare, but most wear old felt hats. They are inured to the African sun; but since the white man wears a hat, the negro wants one too. The door of the Doctor's room opens, and the Doctor appears. He brings out the precious tools that must be so carefully guarded. They have a way of disappearing if they are not counted and kept under lock and key. He returns to fetch the pails from his bedroom, he unlocks a chest on the veranda, he takes out the machetes, the picks and shovels for the morning's work.

Mlle. Maria, the competent nurse, calls the roll: Pouloulou, Charles, Zanzou, N'Goma, Efaghe, Boussougou, Idiata, Ingouma, Kassa, Lane, Bikajoume and so on. Then the Doctor assigns the morning's work. The pump has broken. He will have to repair it later, but now the task is to fetch fresh water.

"Il y a de l'eau à chercher ce matin, car la pompe est cassée. Toi," he says, indicating one of the men, "you will take the women that carry the water, the pails and the big tubs, and go with the two pirogues out into the middle of the river to bring back as much water as you can. Remember, it is not a picnic. You will be back in an hour, n'est-ce pas?"

It is a favorite expression of the Doctor's, this "n'est-ce pas." It ends most of his directions to the natives, with a characteristic rising inflection to provoke a response on their part which will tell him that they have heard and understood the order given. Left to themselves they would not give any response; they would go off leaving him in doubt as to whether they heard and understood. This is one of the peculiarities of the *indigène* mentality.

So off they go for the water, those whose duty it is. Now there are other chores to assign. The dry season comes late this year. The sandbanks have not yet appeared. But the waters have receded from the lower garden, which had been flooded throughout the whole of the hot season. So the water plants that have covered it must be pulled up, piled in great heaps, left to dry for a while and then burned. A portion of the garden that has sunk a little must be filled with fresh loam, taken in part from the upper garden and in part from the rich earth where a compost pile has stood. Then the ground must be turned, the beds and paths laid, and the transplanting of plants from the seed beds effected as quickly as possible in view of the tardiness of the season.

Ten men are assigned to the garden, Etienne, the Christian *contre-maître*, being in charge of them.

"Maintenant, au travail!" the Doctor calls in a loud voice, and sends the men ahead of him down the path. He goes behind. If he led them down the path, a few of them might disappear on the way.

He sets the men to work in the lower garden. Every yard of concrete retaining wall he has built himself. Every cubic foot of soil he has brought there from the kitchen middens of the old native village on the top of the hill left there generations ago. The men are directed to dig the earth from a path in the upper garden and to transport it to the lower garden.

All the while the Doctor is chatting with me he is watching the men at work. Suddenly he stops and picks a weed out of the earth.

"Etienne," he calls, "see that all of these weeds are picked out of the earth. Every one, n'est-ce pas!" Then to me:

"They are the most pernicious weeds in the garden. Look at these long roots with the many nodules. They will kill everything in the garden if I do not get them out."

A long pirogue passes. A man sits in the middle of it. He has four children as pagayeurs. A tawdry rag flies like a pennant from a little stick in the prow of the dugout.

We reach the pump near the riverbank. The Doctor works the handle. It moves too easily up and down.

"I think it's the washers," he concludes. "That will not take so long. But I must go and get my tools."

When the pump is repaired and the tools put back in place, the Doctor can finally give his attention to the work that waits for him at the hospital. He can rarely give himself to it uninterrupted from the beginning of the morning. Almost always he has to busy himself with something else first, perhaps some locks that aren't working, a pirogue that is leaking, metal roofs that need to be repaired, beds that are broken, roads washed out by floods, posts and planks that have to be replaced because termites have got into them . . .

An orderly suddenly appears. The Doctor is wanted in the operating room for a consultation. He hurries off.

Noon. The sun shines fitfully through the clouds. The heat mounts from the earth and the river is shrouded in a yellow haze. From over the river the bells of the Catholic mission sound, and the harsher clang of the Hospital gong responds to it. The work of the morning is done. It is now the time for lunch and rest. The staff comes in from their several duties, Dr. Kopp, Dr. Brach, Mlle. Koch, Mlle. Elise and Mlle. Maria from the Hospital, Mlle. Mathilde and Mlle. Paulette from their many household duties, and Hedi from the garden and the kitchen. There are other guests at the table, a woman expecting her baby, with her husband and little girl, a man who is rejoicing in the arrival last night of a son. All the white patients who are not obliged to stay in bed eat at the Doctor's table. In the center of the long side of the table Dr. Schweitzer takes his place, his wife by his side.

In a very soft voice, hardly audible, he says the grace: "Bénissons l'Éternel, car il est bon, et sa miséricorde dure éternellement."

"BUSINESS DISTRICT"

This is the principal "business district" of the Schweitzer Hospital community. On this compound is the Doctor's headquarters, and also the headquarters of his chief assistants. There is a bustle of activity here from sunrise to long after sundown. People hurry back and forth on urgent errands. Sewing machines stitch noisily. Questions, answers and instructions are called back and forth. Pet monkeys and parrots chatter. Many chores are done in the open. At the far end is the laundry, and to one side are the staff kitchen and the tinsmith shop. In the miniature smithy, a white patient does repairs on hospital equipment ranging from delicate surgical tools to battered fruit pickers' buckets.

Every door in this central compound, as well as in other staff buildings, is locked. In fact everything portable in the whole Hospital community is kept under lock and key. When a native workman needs some nails he must go to "le grand Docteur," who unlocks a storeroom and hands them out. Every time a nurse leaves her room for a short errand, she automatically locks the door. In the home village, there are so few private possessions that the Western man's notion of sanctity of property is just not understood. If some Schweitzer property disappears, the bland explanation is: "It walked away."

MAIN STREET

This is the "Main Street" of the Schweitzer Hospital. There is a bustle of activity here from daybreak to curfew, with a constant stream of foot traffic between the wards and the various Hospital buildings.

The patients waiting to be operated on are housed in a building on the left. Across the street is the main Hospital building, housing the surgery, consultation rooms, maternity delivery room and pharmacies. In the foreground are, on the left, the ward for patients of the Galoa tribe, the somewhat more civilized and gentle downriver peoples; and, on the right, the ward for Pahouins, the people of the upper river.

Patients of other tribes are housed in additional buildings.

During World War II, these buildings were a haven of refuge for *indigènes* and Europeans of the neighborhood (most popular spot: the heavy concrete cistern). Fortunately the Hospital had a good stock of extra-heavy corrugated iron, and this was used to reinforce the wooden walls of the buildings as protection against stray bullets. Crews of aircraft of both the de Gaullist and Vichy forces, which were contending for the village of Lambarene, scrupulously obeyed orders from their leaders not to endanger the Hospital. The victors were the forces of Free France.

The Doctor is in very good spirits, and his humor is infectious. One would never suppose that he had only three hours' sleep last night and only four hours' sleep the night before. Last night he worked on his correspondence and his papers until after midnight, spent two hours in the delivery room with the woman who was having her baby, and as usual got up at six. He himself marvels that, at his age, he is still able to work so well. "It is a grace," he says.

The lunch passes happily. Then the Doctor goes to a table in the corner where the coffee is poured by Mrs. Schweitzer, and for twenty minutes he reads something from the newspapers and illustrated magazines that come from Europe and the U. S.

One o'clock. The hour of the siesta.

"Come," says he, "the siesta is obligatory here. Without it we could not work."

I linger for a moment to speak to someone and the Doctor leaves the dining room. A few moments later as I pass his room I see him sitting at his table, busy with his correspondence. He is not taking any siesta himself today. There are important orders for medicine to be made, with all the papers that the demands of an import license make necessary.

Everywhere there is quiet now. The sun is high in the heavens, stifling, parching. But a little wind begins to blow, the welcome wind of the dry season, which brings the freshness of the winter of the Southern Hemisphere. The courtyard in the quarter of the whites above the Hospital is silent, except for the chatter of the weaverbirds and the clucking of the hens.

At two o'clock the roll of the workers is called again, and one by one they respond. Some of the men are assigned to pick the oranges.

N'Goma ventures to object. "The trees are full of ants, Docteur. They bite us."

The Doctor fixes him with piercing eyes. "You can argue with your wife, you can argue with the chief of the tribe, but you can't argue with the old Doctor. Allez, to the orange trees!"

The workmen are all assigned to their chores. The Doctor starts down the hill to the main Hospital building, and I follow him. Three or four times a week he spends the entire afternoon in his special clinic. After a half-hour of the tense concentration that surgical operations demand, he found he could not see the sutures he was using. But he still takes charge of all certain cases, and does whatever is necessary to relieve them.

On the way he calls to a black man, "Alors, ça va?"

"Un peu, Docteur."

The native always says "un peu" when he means "très bien."

"You have no more trouble?"

"No, Docteur. Thank you, Docteur."

The Doctor's eyes light with a gleam of pleasure.

"Didn't I tell you I would fix you up?"

"Yes, Docteur. Thank you, Docteur. Thank you, Docteur."

We go together to a basement room, doors and windows screened, dark and dingy.

"They call this the submarine," he grins. "If someone asks where is 'le grand Docteur,' they reply, 'He is in the submarine.'"

Inside are five or six high, long tables. Dark faces watch the Doctor attentively, waiting for the help that he alone can give.

"I think you are going to bring me luck today," he says with a twinkle in his eyes, as he begins with his first patient.

"This won't hurt," he says.

Sometimes it does.

"We'll have you around again in no time."

A patient comes in to report.

"I'm all right now, Doctor."

"There, you see. I treated him for four days, and now he is getting on well. It takes a lot of experience in this work."

He is busy all the time.

"Ah," he exclaims, "I knew you were going to bring me luck today. This man will be all right now."

So in the simple room, which would be scorned by any American or European physician, the work of mercy goes on.

The work in the "submarine" ends. Now comes a moment to visit again the dispensary, where a plain wooden table in the corner of the main room is his only Hospital office. There are prescriptions to be filled, medicine to send to white patients seventy miles and more away. The drugs must be prepared, careful directions written out, arrangements for the delivery of the package made. This is not a country of frequent and regular mails and express services. A pirogue with its pagayeurs, a passing pinasse on the river, must serve. Sometimes there are a half-dozen prescriptions to fill.

The day is drawing on. The refreshing breeze of the early afternoon has died away. The time has come for a little respite from the heat of the day. But first the Doctor must see how the men are getting on with the oranges—and the ants. In the orchard above the Hospital buildings we come upon a little group of excited natives. They are not picking oranges. No, they are having a palaver at the foot of the ladder. There is Boussougou again. When he came down from his palm trees, he found that someone had taken twenty-five francs from his pagne. At least that is what he claims. And now he is demanding that Efaghe and N'Goma empty their pockets to show what money they have. They spread out their money. Boussougou claims that he recognizes a five-franc note and a ten-franc note as his. They insist that they have just been paid and that the money is their own. There is much talk and many expressive gestures. It is typical

MANY HAPPY RETURNS

In this isolated community, thousands of miles from the homes of the European and American staff members, birthdays become events. This is the natal day of one of the nurses, and, early in the morning, the staff gathers outside her room to sing chorals from the hymnbook. Then all crowd into her room to offer congratulations. Also, the birthday celebrant has eggs to eat in the dining hall—in memory of the grim early days of the Hospital's existence, when eggs were such rarities that they were saved up for celebrations and festival days.

The Hospital is perennially understaffed, and the overworked nurses and doctors welcome a few minutes' diversion such as this. Dr. Schweitzer has estimated that in the tropics a European can manage to do only about one-half the work he can accomplish in a temperate climate. The requirements of the suffering patients, however, are not adjusted to the work capacity of the staff! They labor long hours, and then fall exhausted into bed at night. When this photograph was made, they were especially haggard because they had just come through the long hot and wet season, when the climate presses down on them with a suffocating clutch.

COMPANION OF THE YEARS

By the side of Dr. Schweitzer throughout the years has stood his wife. Her modesty is revealed by the fact that she hides her face behind the umbrella. Daughter of a professor of history at the University of Strassburg, Helene Breslau was one of the young people that Schweitzer met during his student years. She became a trained teacher and an experienced social worker. She helped him with his work, he helped her with hers. They were married during his year as an interne, and she prepared herself for more useful collaboration by taking a course in nursing. On Easter Sunday, 1913, the doctor and his wife set sail for Africa, and during the long, hard years that followed her intelligent, devoted assistance was of incalculable value. Her health no longer permits her to remain in Africa for the hot, rainy season, and the occasional separations that now occur are a part of the price paid for the opportunity to serve. Whenever possible Mrs. Schweitzer spends the dry season at Lambarene. At other times she lives mostly in the Black Forest at Königsfeld. Her help with the burden of correspondence is especially valued. The Schweitzer's have one daughter and four grandchildren.

of the palavers, which may arise out of the slightest trifle and go on for hours, or even days. If the subject is important—as, for instance, a dispute over the money paid for a wife—the palaver may last for years. Often at the Hospital the Doctor must serve as judge in settling such disputes; otherwise no work will be done until both sides of the dispute are satisfied.

The Doctor quietly moves away. They have been too excited to notice his presence.

"I am too tired to listen to a palaver today. Let us sit down and talk for a little while."

The Doctor looks down to the river.

"It is beautiful, isn't it?" he says. "See these noble palm trees, how lovely they are! This is the moment of tranquility for me."

We return to our rooms for a quiet period before the dinner bell sounds. The equatorial night falls swiftly.

After the pleasant dinner and the quiet service of worship, the company at the table rises. Most of us, however, linger for a little while to have a cup of tisane flavored with mint or cinnamon. After a little while he comes over to me and says, "Would you like to visit my quarters tonight?" Together we take our lanterns—necessary at night because of the danger of stepping on serpents—and cross the courtyard. Above us, between the dark treetops, the Southern Cross shines, three bright stars and a fainter one.

"Come in quickly," says the Doctor. "Pas de politesse! No ceremony, or the mosquitoes will come in too."

The screen door is shut behind us. The Doctor lights his study lamp. It is a strange room for a world-renowned scholar. Near the door is his bed with the mosquito net hung above it.

"You see, I am always a student. I work in the same room where I sleep."

At the head of the bed are nests of pails. They make a kind of wall there. Paddles stand in the corner, hammers, saws and other tools are under the tier of screened boxes which serves as a kind of filing cabinet for his most precious papers.

"I have to keep these things here," he explains. "Otherwise I would never have them. My bedroom becomes a kind of shed for tools. I have to watch everything. I give out brand-new machetes two feet long to the natives. They give them to their relatives and bring me back used ones eight inches long."

We step into the next room, where stands his famous piano with the pedal attachment, the gift of the Paris Bach Society more than thirty years ago. This is no music salon. I can reach out and touch the shelves behind us, full of old, yellow books and papers. The termites have got into some of them, the humidity has made many of them moldy, but there are all the books the Doctor needs for his writing. The works of the great thinkers are to be found on the bookshelves. I notice some volumes of contemporary philosophy in which the Doctor has made marginal notes. He likes to read with a pencil in his hand, carrying on a "conversation with the author." Chinese and Indian philosophy are well represented on the shelves.

Outside the gong sounds. Half past eight! Curfew! Here at Lambarene the word has its literal meaning. All over the Doctor's Village the little fires are put out, and its dark citizens begin to go to sleep.

We return to the other room and Dr. Schweitzer sits down at his table. He grins as he shows me the plain little wooden bench on which he sits. It has a small, thin cushion on it, but it has no back.

"I worked on this seat without a cushion until I was seventy. Now I permit myself the luxury of a cushion." He brings out another small wooden seat of a similar kind for me, and we sit down together before a littered table. He shows me several piles of letters on his desk.

"Letters to answer," he says with a wry grimace.

The letters are tied together with strings. He picks up one pile.

"This string is green, the color of hope. These are the most urgent letters. I hope to answer them soon."

"But what are the letters you always carry in your shirt pocket?"

"Oh, they are just the latest letters to arrive."

I look with dismay upon the piles of letters and think of the many midnight hours they will cost him, precious hours that should be spent on the third volume of *The Philosophy of Civilization*.

"I notice that all your letters are written by hand."

"Yes," says the Doctor, "I don't use a typewriter, because I can't stand the noise of it. And I can't dictate, so I must write my letters in longhand."

Then his mood suddenly changes. He grins and points to the table at his left, where lie a number of white cloth bags.

"These letters on my desk are not all. Those bags are full of unanswered letters also. What can I do?"

Well, what is there for him to do? Many of the letters will not be answered. The many distant friends who write must understand that when the answers do not come it is not because of any lack of interest. No man could work harder than he to respond with affection and gratitude to his many friends. But there are limits beyond which human strength cannot go.

"You have talked a great deal about my forthcoming book on philosophy. Would you like to see the manuscript?"

He turns to one of the shelves behind him, and pulls down a great pile of paper. Sections of it are tied together with string.

"So that they will not get out of order," he says. "This is the manuscript on which I have worked for a quarter of a century, and it serves as a diary of

EVENING VESPERS

Dinner is always a pleasant affair. Often twenty people gather around the long table, and there are never fewer than a dozen people. Four kerosene lamps cast a pleasant glow on the table. The Doctor's head is bowed a little, his fingers play soundless melodies on the tablecloth. There are many things on his mind. He is probably tired. After the meal is over the table is cleared, but everyone remains in his place. Quiet, devoted, efficient Mlle. Mathilde, who supervises all the household with its multitudinous details, silently places before him his Bible, and the little book of hymns.

The Doctor announces the hymn, gets up from the table, walks deliberately around to the piano and begins to play. The piano is in bad condition. Some of the keys stick. Some do not play. But so skillfully does he use the keyboard that no false notes are sounded and no silent keys are struck.

The hymn is sung (the entire service is in French). The Doctor returns to his place, reads a single text from the Bible in so low a voice that one can scarcely make out his words, "Know that your work in the Lord is not in vain." He repeats the Lord's Prayer, and the vesper service is over.

IN THE AFRICAN NIGHT THE VOICE OF BACH

Swiftly as it does the year 'round on the equator the blazing tropical day turns to night: a soft night, with a round, cool-glowing moon. It is a night with a thousand voices: soft voices; the voices of the African forest.

Suddenly in the night a new voice—there can be no mistake—the voice of Johann Sebastian Bach—incisive, firmly reverent—a voice from the resonant throat of a piano under the fingers of a master.

The visitor from far distant Oregon quietly leaves his room, crosses the clearing, and squats on the ground.

The voice of Bach stops. A half-minute later a stocky, slightly bowed figure comes to the screen door and summons the visitor in. And then into a little room to one side. A room with two antelope fawns in a pen, and a piano with a long bench, and under the bench rows of wooden pedals of the kind that organs have. A dark room. The figure slides itself on to the bench and tugs the visitor to sit beside.

The visitor's brain races: Bach—Albert Schweitzer—greatest living interpreter—European concerts—audiences—applause —and now the forest—the African forest a million miles away on the banks of the river Ogowe . . .

And then Bach speaks again and the African night is music.

my life. Look." He points to a page, the left-hand portion of which is filled with his writing. Along the right-hand margin are listed the places where the writing has taken place.

I read, "Steamship Europe, south of Madeira," and the date; "Steamship America, off the Liberian coast," and another date. Günsbach, Strassburg, Liverpool, Port Gentil—the notations show how far the manuscript has traveled over the continents of Europe and Africa. He turns the pages, telling the story of his travels as indicated on the broad margins.

Suddenly he exclaims, "Ah, you see!" pointing to the torn fragment of a page. "This is a page that Léonie has eaten!" And he laughs loudly.

Again he turns to the shelves and brings down more manuscript, piles upon piles of it.

"The problem is to make a book of 250 pages out of this."

"But who insists that you reduce your work to 250 pages?" I ask in dismay. "Is it the publishers?"

"No, no, no," he chuckles, "I never pay any attention to my publishers. They are all my friends. I insist upon it myself."

"Are you working on the book steadily?" I ask.

"I try to work every evening on it, after the day's work is done," he says; "but, for a month and a half now, I haven't been able to work on it at all, because of a very sick patient, who has demanded all of my time. I shall not be able to finish it until I return to Europe and have some months of quiet at my home. For me that is the most important thing now. I should be heartbroken if I could not finish my book." A fleeting look of concern passes over his face. Then he speaks again. "Well, that's enough of the philosophy of civilization for tonight." The heap of manuscript goes back on the shelves again.

And now he takes a book from his desk and opens it. It is a book in which he records the important events in his life. Visitors also write in it, their impressions of the Hospital, expressions of gratitude for generous hospitality. In it Dr. Schweitzer also records the significant events of his life at Lambarene. I notice with interest and amusement that on the same page are recorded the arrival of Mlle. Lagendijk from Holland and the arrival at the Hospital of the tiny fawn Léonie. Here is an instance of the sincerity of the Doctor's conviction that the human being is life that wills to live in the midst of life that wills to live, that the right to life is sacred, and that all life should be respected. Léonie too is important in the scheme of the universe. She merits a place in the Doctor's diary.

It is time to say good night. On the time of "le grand Docteur" one trespasses with qualms. Yet his hospitality is as generous as his heart. He is reluctant to let his visitor go. He takes down a picture from a wall.

"This is my home in Günsbach. Over here to the right on the first floor is my study. The second and third floors are always reserved for Mme. Martin, who represents me in Europe, and the nurses of the Hospital.

He becomes reminiscent again:

"I remember observing from that study window a man and woman who passed every day along the road. I supposed that they were people of slight means who were coming to the good, but modest inn at Gunsbach for dinner. So one day I spoke to them, and said, 'If you feel tired, do come into my garden and rest, and eat any of the fruit you find there.' So they used to turn into my garden and sit there for a time and sometimes I used to chat with them. One day I went out to walk with them for a little, and behind them came an automobile. I spoke to the lady and told her to look out as a car was coming. But she paid no attention to me. I warned her again, but she simply smiled and said: 'He won't run me down. He is my chauffeur.' It turned out that they were wealthy people who used to go out for a ride every day, and at a certain point descend from the car to take a walk for exercise." The doctor's hearty laugh breaks into a gurgling chuckle.

At last I reach the screen door.

"Good night!" I say.

"Good night! Close the door quickly! Remember the mosquitoes."

I pass out into the courtyard and pause to breathe deeply of the fresh night air. It is one o'clock. After a few minutes the Doctor's door opens and he comes out with his old felt hat on, holding his lantern in his hand. He sees me still standing there, and says, "I have a few patients down below and I like to go down before I go to bed to see how they are getting on. Would you like to come with me?"

"Of course," I say.

The Doctor leads the way down the path to the ward where his patients are. We do not speak for fear of disturbing those who sleep. Quietly we climb the steps into the building and stop by the bunk where his first patient lies. He looks in surprise at the man lying in the bed asleep, and then at another man lying on the floor beside the bed, also asleep.

"Look," he whispers to me. "The sick man is on the floor. This is his attendant lying on the bed. It often happens that way. The attendants also want to take advantage of the opportunity of sleeping on a bed like the white man while they are here."

We walk softly down the row of cots. The lantern light is reflected here and there in dark, sleepless eyes. The Doctor says nothing. We come to the second patient. He is awake.

"How do you feel?" asks the Doctor. He is all tenderness now.

"I have a little pain still, Docteur."

"Is it as bad as it was?"

CONFERENCE TABLE

After the evening meal, when the staff lingers for a cup of tisane and informal conversation, "le grand Docteur" returns to this small table in a corner of the dining hall. Any staff member who wants to talk over a Hospital problem or a personal problem in the relaxed atmosphere of this hour can slip over and sit down beside the Doctor and the parrot. If no one brings a problem to him, the Doctor relaxes for a few minutes, leafing through a magazine. Then he is off to his work-desk.

The appellation, "le grand Docteur," does not mean in Lambarene what it seems to mean. Albert Schweitzer is to them not the great Doctor, but simply the old Doc-

tor as distinguished from the young doctors, "les petits docteurs." Yet the very character of the man seems to have thrown an aura of greatness around the words, and Dr. Schweitzer has become for whites and natives alike the grand man of the Hospital, and indeed of the whole colony. Nonetheless there is a moving humility about the man. He has a normal respect for titles that are well merited, and for people worthily occupying important offices; he does not seek to be crassly original and to emancipate himself from all the conventions and traditions that have their meaning and their rightful place in the ruling order of society.

NIGHT WATCHMAN

When one of our photographs of the Doctor's pelican was published in Life, along with other pictures of the Hospital, the bird became a widely known personage. This is as it should be, because he is one of the prominent personalities in the Schweitzer Hospital community. At six o'clock in the evening he flies ponderously up the slope from the river, and takes his perch over the stairway leading to the Doctor's room. Intruders get a resounding crack on the head from his formidable bill. At six in the morning, having seen the Doctor safely through the night, he flaps down to the river for his breakfast. He conceals himself on the downstream side of a projecting stone wall or tree trunk, and keeps an eye out for schools of minnows. With a thrash of his beak he scoops up the lot of them. He lifts his beak high in the air, while the water runs out of it. Then he swallows his catch and resumes his silent watching.

The pelican emulates Dr. Schweitzer in two respects: fondness for pets and public speaking. The bird has a pet of its own—a friendly sheep. Once in a while he follows his pet sheep and the rest of the flock out to pasture, and then, mounting a stump, orates to them earnestly and with vigorous gesturings of wings and beak—apparently giving his version of the Sunday service.

"No, Docteur."

"I think you'll be better tomorrow. Come and see me in the afternoon."

"Yes, Docteur."

"Good night!"

"Good night, Docteur!"

We go on to the last patient. He, too, is awake.

"Better tonight, aren't you?" says the Doctor.

"Un peu, Docteur."

"I'm very glad." The Doctor is smiling. "Sleep well."

"Yes, Docteur."

"Good night!"

"Good night, Docteur!"

We leave the building and ascend the hill again. As we approach the steps to the Doctor's veranda, Monsieur le Pelican raises his bill in warning and breathes harshly and repeatedly. We pause for a moment.

"I was working late one night with Mlle. Hausknecht, writing letters," the Doctor says. "It was two o'clock. Finally I said, 'Let's stop. I'm tired. I don't think I'll go down to the Hospital tonight. I have only one patient just now. I have given him some medicine, and I think he'll get through the night somehow.' So I went to bed. The next morning at half past six I went down to the Hospital to call on my patient. 'How did you sleep?' I asked. 'Not very well,' he said. 'Why didn't you sleep well?' I asked. 'Because you did not come to say good night!' I was very much touched."

He walks up the steps under the pelican's perch. I walk around the veranda to the other end of the building where my room is.

Overhead the moon shines brightly now. The crickets chant their ceaseless song once more. The fronds of the palm trees whisper above, and down the hillside, toward the native quarters in the neighboring plantation of Atadi, banana leaves are silver in the night.

I return to my room and read for a while. But when I go to bed the light still burns in the Doctor's room. The Doctor's Village sleeps. But the Doctor has work to do.

WIDE PHYSICAL VARIATION IN NEARBY TRIBES

In Equatorial Africa, tribes that live within a few score miles of each other may differ radically in physical characteristics. These two young women are of the same age; their difference in height is characteristic of their respective tribes. The shorter one comes from "upriver"— from the hill country of the interior, where food has always been scarce, and growth has been stunted for uncounted generations. The taller one comes from the rich lowlands between Lambarene and the sea. Here, the natives have thrived, relatively, and have acquired finer physiques and more cultivated manners. Both young women are twenty-seven years of age. The fact that their ages are known is exceptional, for few natives keep such tallies. Those who *do* keep count—especially the elders who have not been to school—are apt to count each dry season and each wet season as a year. The result is that the traveler is astonished to learn that some matriarch or patriarch is 140 years old or more! In spite of the strikingly different biological backgrounds of the young women, they were born and reared in essentially the same pattern of superstitions, fetishes, taboos and fears, and consequently have basically the same outlook on life. Furthermore, their complex social systems are virtually identical.

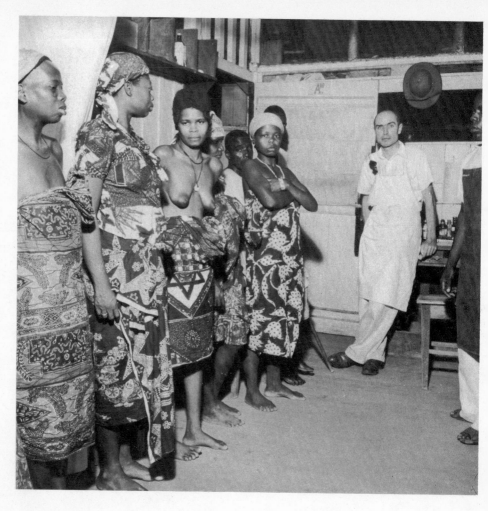

AWAITING DIAGNOSIS

Women from various tribes line up in the smaller consultation room in the main hospital building, for diagnosis of their ills by Dr. Brack, the Swiss physician. The woman who is bare to the waist comes from an isolated inland village. The homes of the others are in more densely populated areas, where there are "Europeans" living. The women in these latter districts follow the lead of Western women in covering their persons.

Diagnosis is made difficult by the patients' confusing descriptions of their troubles in terms of native folkways and superstitions. The patients are expected to bring gifts of kind to help pay for their support at the Hospital, but the Doctor is too tenderhearted to insist on this, and many do not bother to bring anything. Sometimes patients wait for their diagnosis before "delivering." If the diagnosing physician prescribes pills for treatment, then the patient may present the Hospital with a chicken. If injections or surgery are ordered, then a sheep may be produced from the nearby underbrush. However, sometimes the tables are reversed: an occasional patient is under the impression that the Hospital pays for the privilege of treating the sick, and after being cured will present himself to the Hospital's headquarters for his expected fee!

Worms and Their Cure

"Our country devours its own children." An old African chief was speaking to Dr. Schweitzer.

"Here among us everyone is ill," said one of the natives.

There is a naïve idea among civilized peoples that the native of Africa—close to nature, living his simple, active outdoor life, free from all the stress and torment of our complicated, nerve-racking society—must be a very healthy individual; and that even if he is ill he probably suffers less than the white races, who are more refined, more delicate, more sensitive to pain. The logic seems to be that if a people have no dentists, they cannot have a toothache; that if they know nothing of modern medicine, they know nothing of sickness; that if they are not acquainted with surgeons, they need no operations.

This idea indicates the shortsightedness of the white man, his parochialism, his lack of imagination. The damask hangings of ease and luxury conceal the world without, as effectively as do the iron curtains drawn by fear and suspicion.

The native of central Africa knows most of the European diseases, and many diseases that the white man elsewhere does not know. The sun is hot on the equator. Therefore, one has to be more careful of chills than in the temperate zones. During the dry season, so much enjoyed by the European, the native sweats during the day, and shivers during the night, when he sleeps on a thin mat spread on the hard earth. Colds abound. Bronchitis and rheumatism are more common than in Europe. Many of the old people die of pneumonia, the result of camping on the damp sandbanks of the rivers during the annual fishing expeditions.

The principal tropical diseases of the *indigènes* who come to the Hospital for treatment are phagedenic ulcers, framboesia (a form of syphilis), malaria, dysentery and leprosy.

Until 1928 the chief responsibility for fighting trypanosomiasis (sleeping sickness) in the Ogowe region devolved upon Dr. Schweitzer's Hospital. It was for this struggle that Dr. Schweitzer came and founded the Hospital; but after years of labor he became convinced that the problem was too vast for private medicine.

Only government medicine could provide doctors for the necessary yearly visits to all the villages in the vast forest, to interview all the inhabitants, and to examine their blood with microscopes. Only government medicine could maintain a continuous census of all the sleeping sickness sufferers, and could gather them in a central camp to be treated over a period of months. In addition, only the government could require released patients to make regular visits to the doctors who at predetermined times visit local areas, and also force those who suffer relapses to return to the camp.

Says Dr. Schweitzer: "A permanent health control of all the population, and in particular of those who have sleeping sickness, is imperative—and private medicine, of course, cannot exercise this control."

After 1928 the Sanitary Service of the colony took over the task of combating sleeping sickness. Dr. Schweitzer still took part in the fight in the sense that he examined at his Hospital all the patients whom he suspected of being tainted with trypanosomiasis, but if he discovered cases he sent them promptly to the government camp so that they might receive the necessary care from the special staff there.

Free of the tremendous task of fighting trypanosomiasis, Dr. Schweitzer decided to make his Hospital a center of surgical activity, because of the desperate need for such care. Hernias are relatively more numerous here than among the whites. But he could not content himself with operating on the internal hernias of those brought to the Hospital (hernias so advanced, far too often, that it is impossible to save the patient). He found it necessary to do more, and, as far as possible, to take care of *all* the hernias discovered. He sent out word for all *indigènes* with hernias to come to the Lambarene Hospital before they became incurable. As a result, many thousands have been operated on in the course of the years.

In addition to hernias, there are large tumors of elephantisis in men and abdominal tumors in women that necessitate surgical intervention. There are also, in the depth of muscles, abscesses that require operations. Often it is necessary to operate on the same patient five or six times, because numerous abscesses develop anew. Fortunately, penicillin has now come to the aid of surgeons in the treatment of multiple abscesses (which otherwise could weaken the strength of patients to such a point that death would be unavoidable).

Appendicitis operations are very rare in the Lambarene Hospital. They are performed only on the whites; the *indigènes* do not suffer from this illness.

To the operating room of the Lambarene Hospital come numerous victims of accidents in logging camps, natives wounded by savage animals.

Elephants and gorillas are dangerous, as well as the chimpanzees, buffalos, leopards, hippopotamuses and alligators. The hippopotamus, when it is in bad humor, overturns pirogues and pursues its victims in the water, breaking their limbs in its jaws. The buffalo attacks suddenly without provocation.

The leopard becomes especially dangerous when wounded or when pursued by an imprudent hunter. "Leopard-men" also exist in the Equatorial forest, and the *indigènes* fear them as much as the true leopards. These leopard-men belong to a secret society extending throughout all Equatorial Africa. They have become members by initiation rites. Ordinarily, they do not volunteer for membership. Envoys from the society, revealing to them that they are destined to enter it, force them to undergo initiation. The poor creatures obey, knowing that they can do nothing to struggle against the society's reign of terror. Also they believe in the magic powers of those who become members. Once initiated, a member must consider himself as the incarnation of a leopard. He must kill every man and woman named by the society, and he must kill in the manner of a leopard, wearing a leopard skin and armed with leopard's claws of metal. Like the leopard, he must leap upon his victims from ambush. Dr. Schweitzer reports that many deaths have been caused by the leopard-men in the Ogowe region. Although the authorities have done everything possible to discover the chiefs of this terrible association, they are constantly frustrated by *indigènes* who fear to help them.

Venomous snakes are an ever-present threat, but fortunately serums are usually effective. Of course there are exceptions. Since our departure from Lambarene, one of Dr. Schweitzer's workers, Bikajoume, was bitten by a snake on a path behind the Hospital plantation and died within a few hours. Although venomous snakes are numerous in the region, cases of bites are not as frequent as one would suppose. One reason for this is that all the inhabitants, whites as well as *indigènes*, take great care when they walk on the paths or in the grass. They have developed a habit of keeping their eyes on their feet. When walking in the forest, whites are ordinarily preceded by two *indigènes* carrying machetes in their hands. The natives are more experienced in the precautions taken against snakes than are the Europeans, and they are more familiar with the reptiles' habits. At Dr. Schweitzer's Hospital there is one *indigène*, Idiato, who fears no snake. When summoned, he comes running, seizes the reptile by the tail, whirls it into the air, renders it unconscious by hurling it to the ground and finally slashes off its head.

Of all the snakes in the country, the most dreaded is the horned viper. When stretched out on the path or in the grass, it does not stir at one's approach. Because it is short, bark-brown and has no tapering tail, it is readily mistaken for a dead stick. When stepped on, it reacts with the speed of lightning. Its venom is one of the most dangerous that exists.

While jungle animals and reptiles are the most dramatic foes, the creatures that make the most work for the doctors of the Lambarene Hospital are the smallest: the parasites of all kinds. Many children, especially, are brought to the Hospital because of general disability resulting from intestinal parasites.

MAKING THE ROUNDS

The Doctor still makes the rounds of the wards, giving a word of encouragement here, making a diagnosis there. When he was a little younger he insisted on taking the meals to the sickest patients. With twinkling eyes he tells of one such errand. A patient was beginning to convalesce. The Doctor gave him a portion of food that was on the small side. "Is that all I get?" he asked. "Yes," was the reply. "Well, Doctor," said he, "have you anything that I could read?" "Yes, I can send you something," the Doctor said. "All right," the patient returned, "send me a postage stamp to read with my next meal."

The Doctor may prescribe a red medicine, which the patient takes back to his village; when the village fetisher sees it, he throws up his hands in horror. "Red medicine! You can't take that. Red medicine for you is taboo."

A man who has on his leg a phagedenic ulcer as big as a hand is told to keep quiet. He promptly begins to visit all his friends around the Hospital, thus retarding the cure. Likewise in fracture cases the patient gets weary of his immobility and often causes the Doctor great trouble. Yet there is one difficulty the Hospital never has: when the patient is told that he must not work, he finds it very easy to obey. The family supports him.

WAR RECORD

The doctors and nurses, like Mlle. Lagendijk above, agree that they realized the true stature of Dr. Schweitzer during the long years of the war, when the Hospital was desperately understaffed and crippled by lack of medicines. During this time Dr. Schweitzer toiled day and night without complaint, repeatedly taking over the especially disagreeable and difficult duties of the Hospital. "Is it any wonder that we are utterly devoted to him?" asks one of the staff.

During the period when he used to operate, there was often a little ritual at the table after the operation. To understand the ritual, one must remember that local anesthesia was developed in 1892 by Karl Ludwig Schleich, and that his picture hangs in the operating theater. So Dr. Schweitzer used to say to the patient:

"Say thank you to the doctor."

"Merci, Docteur."

"Say thank you to Nurse Elise."

"Merci, Mademoiselle Elise."

"Say thank you to Nurse Pierre."

"Merci, Pierre."

"Say thank you to Bembo, who tied up your hands and feet."

"Merci, Bembo."

"Say thank you to Dr. Schleich."

"Merci, Docteur Schleich."

Then the patient would be released.

Sometimes they are in such a state of weakness that the cure against the parasites is risky.

The primitives believe in worms that do not appear in books of zoology. These are "worms" that spread throughout the human body and cause the most diverse and unfortunate illnesses. The pains accompanying these illnesses are caused by the gnawing activity of the "worms." Thus the aches of rheumatism come from "worms" walking within the feet, the arms, the hands, the back; abdominal pains from "worms" making their home there; and other pains from "worms" in the teeth, the head and the eyes. If the pain of the stomach is succeeded by one in the head, the gnawing "worm" is emigrating from one part of the body to another.

Other serious pains are caused not by imaginary "worms" but by an imaginary animal in the form of a "crab." Many times after an operation the members of the patient's family ask if the doctor is absolutely sure he has found the wicked "crab."

No longer having to concentrate on the fight against sleeping sickness, Dr. Schweitzer is able to give more attention not only to surgical activity but also to the fight against leprosy. In this enterprise he is encouraged by the great progress made by world medicine in recent years. The American Mission for Lepers has placed at his disposal a quantity of two powerful new medicines, promine and diasone. The promine is especially effective in the treatment of the large leprous ulcers which cause such suffering to the patients. Cases of leprosy are numerous in Gabon, and the growing number of lepers who come to the Hospital prove a heavy burden. The difficulty is double: first, Dr. Schweitzer has to be prepared to face the expense caused by the daily feeding of the lepers, and then he has the task of finding the necessary manioc and bananas.

Heavily-reinforced buildings on the grounds reveal the fact that Dr. Schweitzer's Hospital must care for the insane. There is one such building for the *indigènes* and another for Europeans. The principal problem was to achieve strength of construction while providing good ventilation of the rooms in which the insane must be kept in continual confinement, to reduce suffering from the heat. In the villages of the *indigènes*, where there are only bamboo huts, it is impossible to keep the violently insane shut up. The inhabitants often find it necessary to bind the feet and hands of the poor patient, which only excites him more. Not being able to bear his shrieks day and night, the villagers may get rid of him by throwing him in the river. Or, as is more common nowadays, they may take the fellow to the Lambarene Hospital.

Last year Dr. Schweitzer was busy day and night for months with a young European war veteran who was suffering from paranoia. Dr. Schweitzer assisted him with dressing, ate with him, and took him on walks twice daily accompanied by two *indigènes* attendants. Dr. Schweitzer believes from experience that a white insane person ought not to be left by himself for an instant or even with the best *indigènes* attendants. He finds that a white insane person is almost invariably demoralized by being alone with the *indigènes*. While we were at Lambarene the condition of the young veteran was so improved by his care there that he was able to leave the Hospital to travel, accompanied by a friend, back to Europe.

When a patient appears at the Hospital, difficulties at once arise. The disease must be diagnosed. There is the problem of six or more major languages, which is, of course, solved by interpreters. There is the problem created by the strange native ideas of sickness. The native's description of his trouble is often picturesque, sometimes even poetic, but seldom very accurate—as when a village chief said of a woman who was deaf and dumb, "This woman speaks with the eyes, and hears with the heart."

Into the consultation room, where the Doctor sits, comes a native.

"What is your name?" asks the Doctor.

"N'Zamboue." The Doctor writes it down.

"Where do you live?"

"Medemgogoha." This is a village three hours up on the Ogowe River.

"What is your tribe?"

"Pahouin."

"How old are you?"

"I don't know." Birth records are almost nonexistent.

"Have you been here before?"

N'Zamboue lifts up his chin and opens his mouth. "E," he says. He has been there before.

"How many years ago?"

"Five and two years." He can only count up to five; he means seven years ago.

"Where is your card?"

The native finds a dirty card hung around his neck under his pagne and hands it over. It gives his hospital number and all the information already obtained. The Doctor turns to the file and under the year 1940 verifies the record. Yes, there is N'Zamboue. He had been treated for sleeping sickness with tryparsamide, the specific for this disease.

"What is your trouble now?"

"Worm, worm come back again." The repetition of a word turns it into a plural.

"Not the same worms." The Doctor is incredulous.

"M'foghe, M'foghe!" N'Zamboue lifts his fingers in the air. It really is true, he insists.

"How do you feel?"

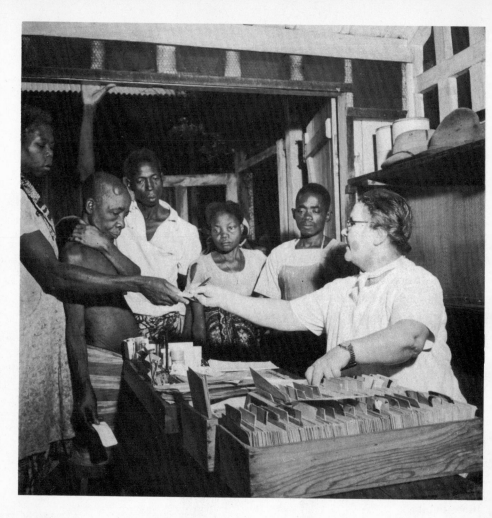

CHARTED

The Schweitzer Hospital may be deep in the wilderness, but it keeps the necessary records of its patients with the conscientiousness of a big city hospital. The Hospital has all the record-cards of the thousands and thousands of patients who have come to it since 1913. All patients are given numbered cardboard tags with strings to tie around their necks. They treasure these tags, and proudly produce them if they have to make a return visit.

Often the forenames of the natives are strange. Christian names are common for those whom the missionaries have baptized. Sometimes these names reflect the date of birth. One little girl, born on the Swiss national holiday, August 1, was called Helvetia. One was called La Crise, a name that the mother explained by saying that the child had been born during the economic crisis of the 30's. One, born while the mother was ill with malaria, was called Malade. Another, born during the bombing of Lambarene, was called La Guerre. Still another was called Tincture of Iodine. Others were called for those who served them: Doctor Albert Schweitzer, Lambarene, Mademoiselle Mathilde, Mademoiselle Emma and so on. "Mademoiselle," in such cases, is used as a Christian name.

DESPERATION

The desperate need for the Schweitzer Hospital is epitomized in this photograph. The woman on the left has had an eye closed by creeping leprosy. (The Hospital is having heartening results from new injections.) The other woman, whose hair is gray with age, has come to have the Hospital find the cause of vicious pains.

The Doctor's efforts in behalf of such patients are greatly complicated by difficulties that arise from ignorance and disobedience. A patient on a severe diet because of intestinal sutures gets tired of his fast, and secretly eats a substantial meal the day after his operation. Almost all the patients try to feel the wound under the bandage. If they are so inclined, they will take the bandage off and wash the wound, or sneak off at night for a cooling bath in the river. A woman will sometimes get drinking water for her sick husband, dipping a bottle into the river at the landing place where the water is worst polluted. The well is too far away. The problem of the medicines is particularly difficult. Even after the utmost care has been taken in instructing the natives, one is never sure that they will not drink the entire bottle at once to hasten the cure, or eat the salve that was to be rubbed on the skin, or rub in the powder that was to be taken with water.

"I am cold." The Pahouin says he is cold when he is hot, when he has a fever.

"Have you any other pain?"

"Yes, blood go up to my head. My body soft." He has a headache and a general feeling of weakness. "E, worm, worm in my side." He points to the left side of his abdomen.

The Doctor puts his hand against the patient's neck. His sensitive fingers can tell within a fraction of a degree what the temperature is. Yes, the patient has a fever. He makes him lie down on the table and gently feels his side where the "worms" are. N'Zamboue winces with pain. The Doctor traces with his fingers the size and location of the hardened spleen.

The patient has malaria.

The hospital card is filled out with the diagnosis and the prescription. Other arrangements for shelter and food are made, not only for him but for his wife who has come to take care of him. The Doctor sends his patient off to get a dose of quinine.

"Omana sela." For the moment the treatment is finished.

It takes a wise physician to diagnose disease under these conditions. He must be very patient with ignorance and superstition. He must understand the natives and discover how to adapt to native ideas and folkways the wisdom of his profession. It has been learned that one must dispense with most of the intricate modern appliances. This does not mean that the doctor does not know about them; on the contrary, he must be so familiar with them that he knows how to do without them. His practice will be a curious mixture of the old and the new. He will use penicillin and sulfa and promine. The new drugs, as they appear, will be made available to him as quickly as possible. But he will have few modern instruments to diagnose disease, and these will be of the simplest kind. He will have no X-ray, no well-equipped laboratory, no way of making tests for metabolism, no electrocardiograph. He will be greatly limited; he will have to unlearn many old things as well as learn many new ones.

The reason is that the excessive heat and humidity wreck all delicate precision instruments. The exposure meter for our camera ceased to function after four days; it had to be baked in an oven for two nights before it began to work again. The Rolleiflex camera lasted for two weeks before it broke down. It has been found that, half of the time, complicated medical instruments do not work, give false readings and are generally untrustworthy. The Doctor is then compelled to work on his instruments instead of on his patients.

The doctor at Lambarene must learn not to waste medicines and surgical supplies. He must learn to do with five inches of sutures what a European doctor would do with twelve. He must be able to face and to conquer loneliness, discouragements, failure.

Native assistants are, of course, of great help to a doctor, when he knows how to handle them. The natives will do well enough what they are taught to do—nursing, injections, and so on.

The actual work of the Hospital itself begins at 6:30 A.M., when the doctors make their first visits to the sick wards. But it is not until after breakfast that the Hospital enters into its full activity. Then the sick from the Hospital and those who come from outside assemble in front of the consultation room. Under the pillars of the surgical ward they sit on benches or stand about patiently waiting for their turns.

The routine activities of the Hospital are manifold. There are the cases of mental disease to be cared for, the quarantined dysentery patients to be served. There are the deliveries at all hours of the day and night, and the motherless infants that must be brought up on bottles. There are the operating room to supervise, the instruments to be sterilized, the medicines to be prepared and administered, the sores to be treated, the seriously ill to be visited in the wards.

The work is resumed at two in the afternoon. The principal duty then is to treat the serious cases in the wards, and to make whatever examinations and analyses are necessary for an accurate diagnosis. There are often consultations among the doctors.

In view of everything, the success of the Hospital in the treatment of medical and surgical cases is astounding, and the amazement of the natives amusing. An old woman whose discomforts from a heart condition had been relieved by a dose of digitalis found that she could once more breathe and sleep with ease. The medicine had made the worms crawl right down to her feet. "Now at last," she said, "we have a real doctor. He knows I can hardly breathe at night, and that my feet are often swollen, yet I never told him a word, and he never looked at my feet. He is a great magician."

Of course, there is sometimes dissatisfaction with the results. A man had a tooth pulled. Afterwards he complained because the Doctor had made a hole in his jaw and had not put anything in it.

Gratitude is likely to be a measured gratitude. The native, of course, has no idea of the fact that the pills may cost the Hospital vastly more than an operation. Gratitude is really shown by the fact that when the natives are in need they come back again. They send their people to the Hospital with strange and moving messages. One such man sent his wife for treatment with a note someone had written for him in French: "Please search in my wife's body from corner to corner."

When the native leaves the Hospital to go home, he receives a large sack made of coarse canvas in which he can carry the things he will need and which he can use as a kind of blanket during the night. He takes with him some bananas and manioc and rice, and a small bag of salt which he can exchange on the

PROUDEST PATIENT

This is the proudest patient in the Schweitzer Hospital. One of the doctors has decided that an operation is necessary in his case. Scarcely anything more enhances the native's prestige. They clamor to be put under the knife. For one thing, they believe the knife is much more effective than medicine in driving out the Evil Powers. In the early years of the Hospital, relatives of a patient insisted on standing over Dr. Schweitzer to make sure he took something *out* ("there go the Evil Spirits"), and did not put anything *in*.

Sometimes when operations are not indicated the patients are so disappointed that they refuse to take medicines and leave in disgust. If the decision were left to them, they would quarrel among themselves as to who should have the privilege of going first to the operating table. They are much impressed with the anesthetics employed. They say, "The Doctor first kills the sick people, then he cures them, then he brings them back to life again." This is understandable, since, if the native himself has an apoplectic fit, or has fallen unconscious, he says that he was dead. The *indigènes* are amazed after a successful operation for a strangulated hernia to find such great relief. One of them exclaimed again and again, "I have no more pain! I have no more pain!"

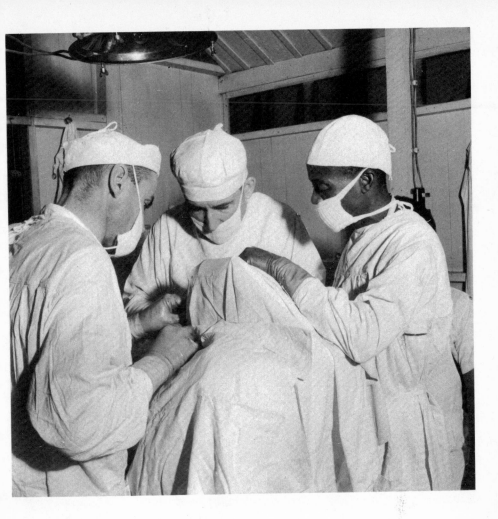

ONE OF THOUSANDS

A staff doctor performs another of the thousands of hernia operations that make up a major part of the surgery schedule. Nearly every family in the region has had at least one case of death from strangulated hernia, and the natives are now coming to the hospital without being urged. In the early years, Dr. Schweitzer and staff members had to go into the surrounding country to educate the natives to call on the Hospital for help. Today there is a festival in the village almost every time a patient goes to the Hospital. Hernia operations in Equatorial Africa are usually much more difficult than those in Western countries because of a greater number of adhesions. While in the West a typical hernia operation requires less than a half-hour, those in Equatorial Africa require on the average two hours, leaving patients and staff exhausted.

The Hospital staff is unable to explain some of the phenomena of an African surgery. Western patients almost invariably, no matter what their present language, babble the tongue of their infancy when undergoing anesthesia. The natives of Equatorial Africa, in contrast, babble not their native dialect but their adopted Western language of French. This holds true even with a primitive bushman who knows only a dozen words of French.

way for other food, and which he can use to pay for his transportation across the rivers. So he goes back to the dark forest which is his country, to the endless palavers and the simple existence with his family and his friends that make life, at least for him, rich and beautiful.

Over all these activities, manifold and beneficent, "le grand Docteur" watches. Whether the ministrations lead to life or to death, everything is his abiding concern. He is haunted by the ocean of need in the midst of which his little island of mercy rests. He sees the work of the Hospital expanding, the faithful doctors and nurses growing old in the service; the burden of financial responsibility weighs heavily upon him. It is his imagination, his vision, his foresight, his consecration, his ceaseless care that spread above this community in the African forest.

PATIENT AND HELPMEET

This middle-aged man has brought his younger wife along to the Hospital to care for him. She is constantly by his side, sleeping at night on the mat beside his bed. She cooks the Hospital's rations of bananas for him and prepares his other food. During the sweltering afternoons, she sits patiently on the side of the bed and fans her husband. This man is relatively prosperous: he has two wives, and has brought to the Hospital an expensive giraffe-design blanket. He also has brought two raffia mats—one to put on the floor for his wife, and the other to lay over the straw in the bed.

If this man is typical of the *indigènes*, he has come to the Schweitzer Hospital only after trying native remedies. Hundreds of different roots, barks, and leaves are used in the treatment of disease. Many of these remedies irritate the kidneys. Others irritate the heart. Cases of delirium have been known to arise from the use of these potions. Some of these drugs are reported to have a strange power about which the white doctors know little. The natives are rumored to give drugs to elephant hunters which prevent them from seeing anything but elephants. Other drugs are said to exist which make it possible for a man to travel all day long without thirst and without fatigue.

WILDERNESS STAFF

The major work of the Hospital is divided among the three doctors and the three nurses who are assigned to special responsibilities. (Names change from year to year, but we list the staff as of the time we photographed them, and give their stories in brief because they will be, in large part, representative of future doctors and nurses.) There is Dr. René Kopp (far left), the competent chief surgeon, from Münster, where the family lived about a mile from Dr. Schweitzer's home. As a boy he knew Dr. Schweitzer, although he was much more interested in the Doctor's large black dog than in the man whom he was to serve later. Dr. Kopp comes from a minister's family, and was long interested in the heroic story of Livingstone. So it happened that he gave up his pastorate in Alsace, and, following Schweitzer's example, studied medicine and enlisted for service in Africa. But he is still a pastor, and every few weeks he preaches at the simple Sunday service. He is to the natives "le petit docteur," not because he is small in stature, but because he is younger than Dr. Schweitzer. His attractive and able wife (left, front row) assists in many ways.

There is Dr. Arnold Brack (right, second row), the devoted junior surgeon, who gave up his practice in Zürich, and came to Africa to help. He had known Dr. Schweitzer by his books for some twenty years, and now finds the work at Lambarene exceedingly interesting. He is also "le petit docteur," and so the natives have to distinguish him from Dr. Kopp. This they do by gestures, imitating the different ways in which the two doctors wipe their foreheads when it is hot, the latter with an upward thrust of the hand, the former with a sideways motion.

There is Mlle. Gertrud Koch (directly in front of Dr. Brack), who, as early as 1918, knew that one day she would go to Africa. After hearing Dr. Schweitzer lecture she knew that she would work with him. She has still the same enthusiasm as at the beginning and hers is a genuinely Christian motivation. While troubled by the changes that have occurred in the natives since the war, she goes on with the work without futile complaining, without looking backward.

There is Mlle. Elise Stalder (second from right, front row), a Swiss Red Cross nurse, who assists in the operations and takes charge of all the sterilization, and of the purchasing and distribution of food.

There is Mlle. Maria Lagendijk (between Dr. Schweitzer and Dr. Brack), who always wanted to go to the most primitive region in the world, and decided that this was Gabon. She is partly responsible for the care of the white patients, but helps in many other ways, with fruit-gathering, with the correspondence and with other chores. Friendly, lovable, and versatile with her language and her skill, preaching occasionally at the Sunday services, she too has an indispensable place in the Hospital scene.

There is Mlle. Mathilde Kottman (far right), who has been here longer than any of those pictured except Dr. Schweitzer himself. She is responsible for the multitudinous details of the housekeeping, and is in charge of the garden, plantation, the chickens and the sheep. Her quiet and devoted efficiency make smooth in the jungle the highways of service.

Junior nurses shown in the photograph are Hedi Meier (between Dr. Kopp and Dr. Schweitzer) and Paulette Crevoisier (second from left, front row).

In Alsace at the time of this photograph was Mlle. Emma Haussknecht, who has been in the Hospital service since 1935.

The natives have difficulty with foreign names and so rename in their own way all members of the staff. One former tall physician was called "Long, Long, Long." Another very energetic one was called "The Tornado."

COURAGE AS WELL AS COMPETENCE

The *indigène* medical staff is a source of immense pride to Dr. Schweitzer. Nearly all have been trained at the Hospital. They have overcome almost overpowering handicaps of superstition and local pressure. Some have risked retaliation by home villagers. They all know of predecessors who have paid with their lives for working at Lambarene.

Dr. Schweitzer states firmly that some of these staff members may properly be regarded as "truly remarkable." He adds: "Their work is so vast, so varied and so complicated that they come to be indispensable."

In a colonial hospital such as Lambarene,

there are so many patients for each staff member that every possible shortcut must be worked out. For example, temperature charts are kept only for those patients whose ailments require such information. Because of the shortage of staff, the doctors are accustomed to many tasks which elsewhere are delegated to attendants.

The medical assistants are nearly always men. The Hospital finds it almost impossible to get women nurses (note one exception above) because the native girls marry at such early ages. (Many, in fact, are bound in a marriage contract when they are infants.)

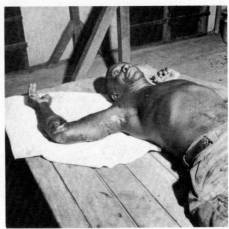

THE KIND OF PEOPLE THEY SERVE

Above: This young wife has but a few more weeks to live. She is another of the tragic incurables who come to the Hospital. Consoling her is her husband, who came to Lambarene to cook her food and attend to her.

Below: Framboesia sores mar the skin of this child. These strawberry-like sores are associated with the particular kind of syphilis encountered in Equatorial Africa. It strikes the innocent—the sores appear in the children of infected parents. If the child stays at the Hospital long enough for the full series of treatments, he will return to his village cured.

Above: A male gorilla, thinking the three female gorillas with him were in danger, attacked this workman in the forest; but, although unnerved, the man was able to make his way to the Hospital for treatment of his wounds. The gorilla characteristically makes one pass at his victim and then flees. In this case the animal's claws mauled the man's right arm and the brute's jaws came down on a thumb. The workman considers himself lucky. Not many escape so lightly.

Below: With his shriveled leg in a cast, this boy must reconcile himself to a long stay at the Hospital.

SOME DO SHOW APPRECIATION

There are exceptions to the usual *indigène* attitude of taking the Schweitzer Hospital for granted. Some patients do show gratitude. When our pirogue put in momentarily at the village of N'genge Zone on the Ogowe, this girl rushed down to the shore to greet Nurse Maria, who had treated her for malaria and hookworm. Whenever members of the staff travel in the region, they find former patients in nearly every village. The sight of these people, cured of ills that in many cases would have been fatal if untreated, is a profound source of encouragement for the hard-working nurses and doctors.

Nurse Maria remembers that the most moving expression of gratitude came from a mother living in another village. This woman told her: "I go to the Protestant Mission now, every Sunday. When I was sick, you stayed with me late at night, and comforted me when my baby died. The European God must be better than our God."

Other *indigènes*, however, find it impossible to understand why, if God is compassionate, He has allowed the whites to come to rule over them. The Europeans explain that God makes no distinction among skin colors and that, after all, the Europeans *have* suppressed cannibalism and intertribal warfare.

NEEDLE SPECIALIST

Three times a week injections are given at the door of the consultation room. One of the nurses makes the rounds of the Hospital ringing a cowbell, to call the lepers, the tubercular, the syphilitic, the victims of elephantiasis. It takes about an hour to assemble them all. One by one they are called for their injections, given by this competent native nurse who is able to find the smallest and most inaccessible vein with his needle. When the list is called there are always missing ones, away bathing, or fishing, or gathering fruit and nuts and wood in the plantation and the forest. So the nurse has to round them up one by one. Often some recalcitrant who has spent the entire day away from the Hospital comes back in the afternoon to complain naïvely that he has not had his injection.

Here, the deadliest of enemies are the insects: the malaria-carrying mosquito; the tsetse fly, bearing sleeping sickness; the red fly with the threadworm eggs it imbeds in the eye of an animal or human. (A Swiss surgeon who spent several years assisting Dr. Schweitzer could not rid himself of the threadworm until ten years after his return to Europe.) One can usually avoid the animals. There is no way of escaping the myriads of disease-laden insects.

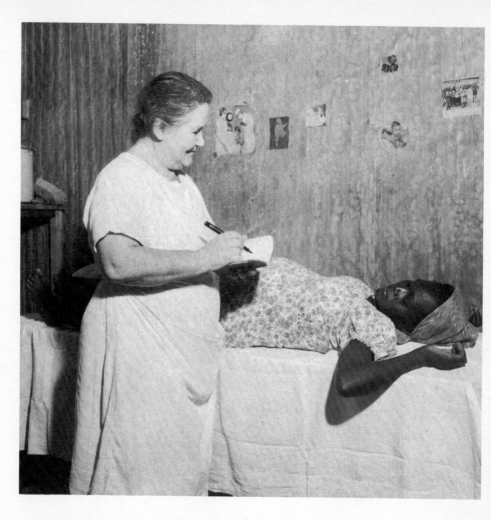

VOTES OF CONFIDENCE IN THE HOSPITAL

More and more women are coming to the Hospital to have their babies. This is especially true with younger mothers. They know the infants' chances of living are much greater than in the case of deliveries in native huts. Nowadays the mothers-to-be willingly permit, in most cases, even the assistance of the men doctors. In former years there was a great deal of difficulty because the mothers thought that the Evil Powers would punish the mother and child if any man attended the birth. Even today there are a few cases of mothers who come to get hospital care before and after childbirth but, fearing that a male doctor may help in the

delivery, steal off into the bush and then carry the crying infant into the Hospital. The peak month in the number of births is March, while in Europe it is June.

The present confidence in the Hospital is in marked contrast with Dr. Schweitzer's experience in the early years of the institution's existence. In the tropics, it is necessary to have graves prepared in advance, so that interment can be immediate. One of the early warnings whispered among the *indigènes* was: "Don't go near the Hospital. You'll surely die. They have your grave all ready for you." One of the strongest superstitions is that preparation for death tempts fate.

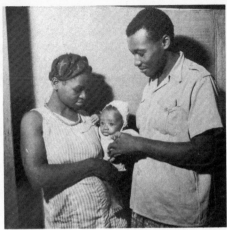

BABIES . . . BABIES . . .

Above: This male nurse has a special knack with babies, and he is kept busy the day long giving them their bottles, bathing them and quieting them.

Below: This mother is unable to nurse her baby adequately, so she has brought her child to the Hospital for help. The nurses prepare a special formula with powdered milk from America. Mother and child will stay in the Hospital until the baby is six months old and can take soft foods. Meanwhile, the staff will teach the mother how to make soup from bananas, and how to prepare rice, papaya and other foods for infant consumption.

Above: This mother has an inadequate supply of milk, and is staying on at the Hospital so that her baby will have supplementary feeding. This maternity ward was built and supplied with money raised by Mlle. Koch with lectures in Europe while recuperating from the Equatorial climate.

Below: One of the nurses shows the young mother the proper way to bathe a tiny infant. The loose string is tied to the arm, neck or waist of many babies in accordance with a superstition that it will keep away the Evil Spirits so long as worn without being loosened.

MAMMA'S BOYS (AND GIRLS)

In Equatorial Africa, a child literally and completely belongs to the mother's family. When the child falls sick, the father has nothing to say about what shall be done. It is the wife's mother, or her brothers, who decide whether the child is to be treated by native medicine men or is to be sent to the Schweitzer Hospital or to a mission doctor. When a boy reaches his teens, he is turned over to one of his uncles for rearing and training.

One reason the adult natives are so irresponsible is that they were never effectively disciplined as children. Neither father nor mother nor grandmother nor uncle will lay a hand on a child, because that would bring the Evil Powers to take revenge.

These mothers, representative of those found in the wards, have great confidence in the ability of the staff, but they have one persistent fear: the birth of twins. According to the native superstitions, the same spirit cannot be in the two bodies. If the twins are a boy and a girl, then the boy will usually be starved (the girl can be sold for cash); if two boys, the weaker one will be starved. The parents have nothing to say about this; the villagers will take matters into their own hands, to ward off the vengeance of the Evil Spirits from the whole settlement.

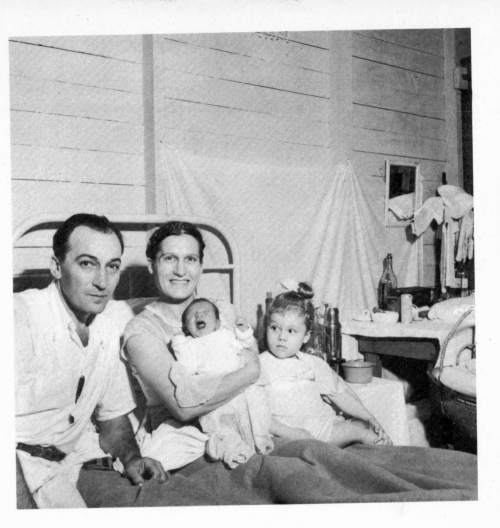

HELP FOR THE 5 PER CENT

Even though about 95 per cent of the Hospital is devoted to the care of *indigènes,* the Hospital fills a desperately needed role in the case of the European settlers. They, too, come hundreds of miles to have the lifesaving benefits of the Hospital. Mothers need not always face the grim prospect of childbirth in the dark reaches of the equatorial forest. They are always made warmly welcome by the staff of the Lambarene Hospital.

This mother was formerly a nurse at the Schweitzer Hospital. After several years' duty, she married a French timber operator and moved deep into the interior. She came to the Hospital for the birth of her first child, and has returned for her second, who is seen lustily greeting the new world.

This and other European families look upon the Hospital as "home," and come to it to spend the holidays. The Doctor chuckles and says that he can tell when Christmas is coming by the arrival of friends from the interior. Their presence helps relieve the monotony of the existence at Lambarene, and, of course, they reimburse the hospital for their expenses. The visitors join the staff at meals in the communal dining room, and often help out by doing chores or by transporting supplies in their boats.

CONSULTATION ROOM: FOR PATIENTS; FOR CIVILIZATION

"Le grand Docteur" is at his desk in the crowded consultation room of the main hospital building. Here he tends to patients' needs, and here he snatches, when he can, some spare minutes to do a little more work on *The World-View of Reverence for Life*, the third volume of his series, *The Philosophy of Civilization*.

In the first part of this work he has written[*]: ". . . I have come to the conviction that the aesthetic and the historical elements, and the magnificent extension of our material knowledge and power, do not themselves form the essence of civilization, but that this depends on the mental

[*] Quoted by courtesy The Macmillan Co.

disposition of the individuals and nations who exist in the world. All other things are merely accompanying circumstances of civilization, which have nothing to do with its real essence. . . .

"Creative artistic, intellectual and material attainments can only show their full and true effects when the continued existence and development of civilization have been secured by founding civilization itself on a mental disposition which is truly ethical. . . . If the ethical foundation is lacking, then civilization collapses, even when in other directions creative and intellectual forces of the strongest nature are at work."

WHERE FORESIGHT SAVES LIVES

The pharmacy is Dr. Schweitzer's special responsibility. It is a heavy one. Drugs must be available for long months ahead. Bottles, tin boxes and glass tubes must be procured. All such things are so hard to get that the Doctor has to be a hoarder. At a recent birthday celebration, he gave his picture to one of the staff in an envelope tied with a ribbon. After the gifts had been opened the Doctor called down the table, "You can keep the picture, but I want the envelope and the ribbon back!"

So the Doctor watches over his pharmaceutical supplies. All medicines must be put into metal boxes which are proof against the terrible humidity and the equally formidable, omnipresent termites.

The scarce drugs and hospital supplies must be rationed, stretched out over a longer period, hoarded and guarded, for they mean life and they are often irreplaceable. There is the precious promine, for instance, from the American Leper Mission, with which the Doctor has such encouraging results. Last summer he had only enough for forty lepers. When and where was he to get more? There are many thousands of lepers in the vicinity.

The Doctor is here shown in the main pharmacy, where the most frequently used drugs are kept, preparing medicine for a European who is stranded in the forest.

JOURNEY OF HOPE—AND OF DESPAIR

One bright morning two young people arrived at the Hospital, man and wife. They belonged to the distant Bahanjegi tribe; they had come three hundred miles on foot and by pirogue to have an enlarged thyroid gland on the woman's neck removed. Because of their having come such a great distance, I promptly photographed them when they arrived. Marie Louise Zandji had been to the Hospital eight years before to have a thyroid removed. The thyroid had come back again. A few days later I photographed the operation itself. It was a difficult operation and the patient lost much blood. But nonetheless she came through it successfully and was taken to the surgical ward. A few hours later Dr. Kopp was suddenly called to her bedside. An embolism had developed and although every emergency method was tried the girl died.

That evening in the little shed where her body was laid her husband was beside himself with grief. Wringing his hands and lifting them to the sky, he sobbed and cried and chanted:

My wife does not speak to me.
She does not open her eyes.
She does not come back any more.
She is dead.
Death is like the moon.

There will always be a moon.
There will always be death.

Then at last in utter exhaustion he threw himself on the ground beside the simple bier, put his arm over the dead girl and sobbed himself to sleep.

Early the next morning the little funeral procession went up the hill. In accordance with native customs, the husband did not go with it. But his friends carried the body on a stretcher, and Dr. Kopp accompanied them for the simple, beautiful service. Reverently the body was committed to the ground, the coffin (fashioned by friends from half of an abandoned pirogue)

covered with a white cloth, on the top of which a single palm branch had been laid—the symbol of victory over death. Quietly the body was lowered into the grave, solemnly the minister threw three shovelfuls of earth upon it. It was a moving little service, particularly because the doctor who had failed to save the girl's life himself spoke the last words of love and faith over her grave.

The next day the husband slipped away. There was no word of complaint, no word of gratitude. He knew the white doctors had done all they could for his wife, but they had not saved her, so there was nothing to thank them for.

THE BATTLE WITH GERMS IN THE DARK CONTINENT

Cleanliness and orderliness—to what lengths the Hospital must go, to achieve them!

The wood-stoked fire outside the main hospital building, above, is kept blazing furiously. Surgical instruments are boiled in pans, and kettles are kept steaming to provide sterile water for the operating room. An unusually large number of injection needles must be boiled, because a large proportion of the operations are performed under the influence of spinal or local anesthetics.

On Saturday afternoons there takes place a general housecleaning, for which all the available men and women are mobilized.

The wards and houses, the streets of the Hospital and all the adjoining fields are cleaned of dirt and debris and garbage. Bottles, tins and rubbish are gathered. Dr. Schweitzer says it reminds him of Millet's "The Gleaners." But it is a necessary fight against the mosquitoes that breed in abandoned tins and bottles, and against the malaria they carry.

In the afternoon of the last day of the month there is a complete roll call. Often patients leave quietly without saying good-bye. Others slip in without announcing their arrival. It is necessary to have a monthly check-up. It is an extraordinary spectacle when the whole community, with

the exception of the bedridden, presents itself at one time. First the cards of the bedridden are checked. They have been brought by the native orderlies. Then in groups come the people from the lumbering camps. Afterward the people are called by the regions from which they come: the people from Koulou-Moutou, the people from the upper Ogowe, the people from N'Djole, the people from the Samkita region, the people from the Abanga River, the people from Lambarene, the people from the region N'Gomo, the people from the great lakes, the people from Lake Azingo and so on.

In the picture above, a doctor and a medical aide scrub up before entering the operating room. The initials "ASB" are ubiquitous; they are found on virtually everything that is portable—painted on pirogues and tools and equipment, chipped into enamelware and sewn into clothing. They stand for "Albert Schweitzer-Breslau"—the latter being the maiden name of Mme. Schweitzer. They adopted the initials when they arrived in Africa in 1913. The initials are known throughout the Equatorial African colony. Even packing cases in which fruit is sent to the coast will return, presently, to the Hospital; for everyone knows that property marked "ASB" is to be returned to Lambarene.

END OF A JOURNEY

Weary from six long weeks of cross-country travel, she has just arrived at the Schweitzer Hospital with her husband, who is in danger of losing his life if he does not have a hernia operation soon. They have come from the Bakota tribe near Lastourville—250 miles east. They had to cover half the distance by foot, over rough terrain, before being able to shift to a pirogue. The wife is wearing the raffia pagne of the inland tribes, the use of which has nearly disappeared in the coastal regions.

One reason for the frequency of hernias among the men is that most physical work is done by the women. Hence the men's abdominal walls usually remain weak. Also, when they have plenty of food they overstuff themselves and consequently stretch their abdominal walls.

The wife is burdened down because every patient is requested to bring a mosquito net, a blanket, a mat to lie on and a saucepan. Often they say they have none, but when the Hospital responds, "What a pity, for we haven't either," these necessary articles usually appear.

Three mornings in the week, newcomers are admitted to the Hospital and outpatients are treated. But there are always exceptions on other days—such as on this morning.

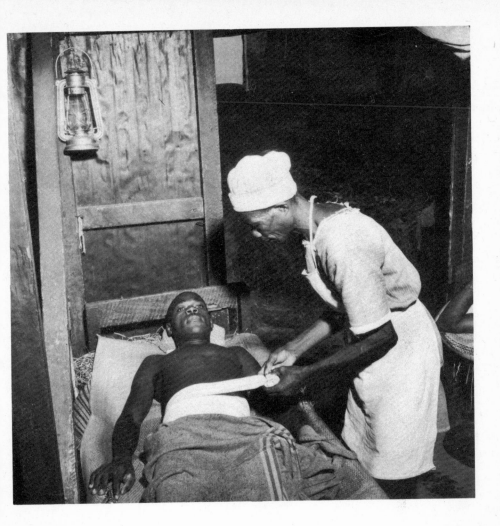

PRIZED MEDICAL AIDE

This is a rare *indigène*—immune from witchcraft. He is not afraid of caring for the most violently ill patients and does not fear the Evil Spirits if death should come. He has a tiny bedroom in the ward of the patients who are either awaiting operations or recuperating from them. Here he is, in the middle of a sweltering tropical afternoon, binding another hernia victim, who is now recovering.

Dr. Schweitzer has described the fiendish hold that witchcraft has on the *indigènes*: "Europeans will never be able to understand how terrible is the life of the poor creatures who pass their days in continual fear of the fetishes which can be used

against them. Only those who have seen this misery at close quarters will understand that it is a simple human duty to bring to these primitive peoples a new view of the world which can free them from these torturing superstitions."

Even those who are liberated from superstition, like this medical aide, must compromise in their native villages. For example, during a death festival, the enlightened ones usually go through the motions of "making tam-tam," putting food on the grave, and otherwise "doing as the Romans do" so that the more orthodox of their fellow villagers will not feel that the Spirits are outraged.

SUMMONS

Sunday comes. It is nine o'clock in the morning. The Doctor leaves his room for the preaching service. On the path just below the dining hall a bell hangs on a tall wooden frame. The Doctor pulls on the chain, and the bell sounds over the roofs of the wards. Its notes reach all who suffer and all who watch over them. This to the Hospital natives is the voice of God calling, the gong that calls them to work each day being the voice of the Doctor. They know that the voice of God must also be heeded. If they are well enough to move about, they need go to the Protestant mission, to the Catholic mission, or to the service here at the Hospital.

As soon as the first bell sounds, every pot must come off its little fire in front of the patient's door. Attendance at the service is not optional. Schweitzer says to the native who seems reluctant to move, "Do you think that when the Lord Jesus preached the Sermon on the Mount he had to go about to all the villages and kick over the pots so the people would come to the service?

The Doctor finds the *indigènes* are interested especially in stories such as those of the Good Samaritan, the Prodigal Son and the Sower, as well as all Biblical fishing parables. These they can relate to their own experiences.

The Feast of St. John

The evening meal is over. The simple service of devotion has ended. There is a little talk around the table as the customary tisane is sipped, flavored with mint or cinnamon. Then we arise, turn up the wicks of our lanterns and go out into the night. This evening, however, we do not go to our rooms; all of us together cross the courtyard, walk around the building where the Doctor lives, past the pen where the adult antelopes are kept, and then down the path that leads through the garden to the river. On the lowest level of the garden some of the natives are waiting for us, and there we find a great pile of wood, mostly branches from the palm trees. It is the Feast of St. John the Baptist. We are to celebrate it, after the fashion of Alsace, with a great bonfire.

The river flows quietly, quickly, in the background. The night sky is bright with stars. The bonfire is lighted. More and more branches are thrown on it, until it rises high above us. The sparks from the crackling wood drift across the heavens, and the brilliant constellations of the southern skies take on strange, uncharted, changing forms. Children's dancing figures are silhouetted darkly against the light until they circle into the ruddy flames on the other side of the fire. We sit and watch and dream.

Albert Schweitzer is there among us. He is silent, very silent. The bonfire brings back memories of his peaceful, beautiful valley, from which he has been so long separated; memories of friends, old and dear, many of whom he will never see again. The years that are gone pass in long procession before him. He is living again in the past. Around him burn the fires of St. John on the tops of his Alsatian hills. The Ogowe flows by unheeded, forgotten.

The Feast of St. John always moves him profoundly, for the great figure of John the Baptist is full of meaning for him. John was the first among men to recognize the significance of the new prophet who appeared on the banks of the Jordan, the first man to die a martyr for the new faith.

Sunday comes. The Hospital, so far as it is possible, rests. The Doctor, however, does not rest. He is to preach, as is his frequent custom. And since it is St. John's Sunday he will preach about St. John. The early prohibition against his preaching, imposed by the Paris Missionary Society because of his "unorthodoxy" when he first came out to Africa, was long ago removed. The obligation of his promise to be as "silent as a fish" has been voided. Neither the Paris Missionary Society, nor any of the other missionary movements, now fears what the Doctor may say—although "unorthodox" he remains. They are grateful that another voice is lifted against the paganism and superstition Africa seems to be drifting back to. And the natives listen gladly to this white prophet, preaching on the banks of a new river of which John the Baptist had never heard.

It takes about half an hour for the natives to gather for the service, down below the hill between the Hospital wards. Here there is no chapel, nothing to suggest a church. No altar or Communion table, no pulpit or lectern, no pews or seats, no organ or piano. The services are held in the open air, between the Hospital wards. Men, women and children gather in the shade of the wide eaves. They sit in the doorways, on the steps that lead to the buildings, on the ground. The people take their places as they please. They do not sit in rows; they sit in groups or singly, and overhead the bright tropical sun shines from a sky more beautiful than stained-glass windows. But the sun is hot. The people cling to the shadows.

This is not much like a church—but neither was the stable at Bethlehem. Here, as there, the animals are at home. The cattle, of course, are absent; the tsetse fly has banished them. There are sheep here, but they are not like the sheep of the Christmas shepherds: these are African sheep, with smooth coats of hair instead of wool. The dogs wander about at will; the goats, the monkeys, the hens and the ducks are at home. There never was a St. Francis that cared more for them than does the Doctor. They are welcome at the divine service. No one disturbs them, even when they take a noisy part in the service. The monkeys may scamper about on the corrugated-iron roof, the dogs may bark at the Doctor's feet, the goats may bleat, the weaverbirds may keep up an infernal chatter in the palm trees overhead—but they have their rightful place here. The Doctor raises his voice when it is necessary.

And the people! What a study in black humanity! Some of them have come long distances by river and jungle trail. Many have never heard Christian preaching before. They roll the whites of their eyes as they watch everything with inscrutable faces. What magic will the white fetisher perform? Others come from the vicinity. They know what to expect, but their faces are as impassive as those of the others. Some of them have been at the Christian missions, and the Catholic converts wear a little medal hanging from their necks. Some come from the once-ferocious Pahouin tribes. Others come from the coastal tribes, the Galoas. Some of the congregation are awaiting operations. Others are convalescing from them. A scrawny old man dances and sings at the end of the little street. He chuckles and laughs. He is very happy. He is insane. A boy limps up and sits on the ground, a huge phagedenic ulcer on the side of his leg. A woman with a goiter sits beside him. Several women bend over their marmites and stir the simmering contents above the little fires. It is against the rule, but everyone pretends not to see; here where the service is to take place they can still do their cooking and listen as well. Several mothers sit in their doorways nursing their babies at big, pendent breasts. Many of the women are naked to the waist; some have their gay, cotton pagnes fastened under their arms.

Dr. Schweitzer picks his way quietly among the groups of natives and stands against the smoke-blackened walls of one of the barracks under the overhanging roof. He is wearing his usual darned khaki trousers, and his white shirt is open at the neck. On his head he wears his white sun helmet. Two natives take their places, one on each side. In their Sunday clothes they are much better dressed than Albert Schweitzer; but for the Doctor religion is something of the heart, having nothing to do with vestments or altar furnishings. Yesterday this place was a rude street between rows of simple hospital buildings. Today it is a church of God, but it is not candles or cassocks that have transformed it. The natives that stand beside him are the two interpreters, a Pahouin and a Galoa. Some of the hearers will understand neither language, for probably a dozen dialects are represented here, but more interpreters would bring confusion into the service.

The services used to begin with the solemn music of a gramophone, but the machine has long since broken down. Now the Doctor begins with the liturgical sentence: "In the name of the Father, and of the Son, and of the Holy Spirit." The Pahouin translates. The Galoa follows. Then a hymn is sung. The congregation has no books, so that it is useless to announce a number. The interpreters begin to sing, and the congregation picks up the tune. Of course, only those who have been in the schools of the Protestant missions and have memorized the hymns are singing. Still, the singing is lusty enough. They have fine voices, these negroes of the plains and the forests.

After the hymn the Doctor prays, his words interpreted sentence by sentence by the black men on either side.

"God our Father, we thank you for giving us this Sunday anew as a day of rest. Help us to celebrate it as it should be celebrated: not only as a day of rest for the body, but also as a day of celebration for our souls. May we this day hear your word, may we open our hearts to your gospel, may we come near you in our prayers, may our spirits rise towards you. Let us not only celebrate the Sunday (the Sabbath), but really make it holy, that we may be turned away from earthly thoughts to occupy ourselves with spiritual things. Grant that, everywhere that Christians are gathered before you today, they may make the Sabbath holy. Let this Sunday be a holy Sunday for us. Grant the strength of thy spirit to thy children."

There is silence everywhere, except for the noise of the animals. Several goats

FELLOW WORSHIPERS

On this Sunday morning, one of the nurses is conducting the chapel service, and Dr. Schweitzer joins the congregation. Staff members conduct the service on alternate Sundays. Perhaps this morning Dr. Schweitzer is recalling to mind the first church he attended as a boy in far away Günsbach. There, Catholics and Protestants worshiped together. As he sat in the pastor's pew, restless as a small boy must be—during the long sermon that rumbled from the high pulpit, filling the little church with sonorous unintelligible syllables—he found something he could understand when he looked through the wooden bars of the chancel screen to the Catholic altar with its towering candlesticks, its artificial flowers and its gilded angels, all flooded with light from the chancel windows. Later he wrote of that experience, "Through the windows themselves one looked out over trees, roofs, clouds and blue sky—on a world, in short, which continued the chancel of the church into an infinity of distance, and was, in turn, flooded with a kind of transfiguring glory imparted to it by the chancel. Thus my gaze wandered from the finite to the infinite, and my soul was wrapped in peace and quiet." That early experience remained for him ever a symbol of religious unity.

"THE HOLY SPIRIT IS LIKE THAT . . ."

Semiliterate and illiterate natives, many of them with a cannibal background, hear the spoken wisdom of this theologian and philosopher. Two medical aides stand on either side of him. The Doctor speaks a sentence in French; one aide translates (with gestures) into the Pahouin dialect, and then the other translates it into the Galoa dialect. Excerpt from this sermon: "Here is the great river behind us. In its upper reaches it is swift and tumultuous. There are turbulent currents and dangerous rapids. It is a savage stream. The river flows onward. The farther it flows the broader and stronger and more tranquil it becomes. The Holy Spirit is like that.

At first there is very little sign of its presence in the savage hearts of men. But little by little it grows stronger and men become filled with it. Then it manifests its force in the hearts of men . . .

"It is difficult, of course, to open our hearts to the Holy Spirit. The Holy Spirit is strange to us. It wishes to control our lives. It wishes to govern us in everything. In little things as in big things. And the sign of the Holy Spirit is the way in which we live. The Holy Spirit would prevent us from killing. It would prevent us from seeking revenge. It would rule our lives even in our own homes. We must seek to possess it."

are eating in a huge bin filled with garbage. Some ducks waddle along in single file between the buildings.

The sermon begins:

"On Tuesday, the twenty-fourth [it is June, 1947], we celebrated together, as you have all heard, the Feast of St. John. Today, as is my custom every year, I will speak to you of the great man who was John the Baptist, this great man of God.

"First I will tell you of his life as it is written in the Gospels, and of his words, as we read them there. The Gospels do not tell us much about him when he was a child. They tell us that when he was a man he began to preach that the kingdom of God was near. Repent, he said, in order that you may enter into that kingdom.

"Then he began to baptize people. He took them to the river and put water on them, just as if he were washing their bodies. Now, he said, you are cleansed of all your sins. Now you can enter into the kingdom of God. So he purified them by this baptism so that they could enter into the kingdom of God.

"Among those who came to him was a certain man. His name was Jesus. When John saw him he said, 'This man is greater than I. It is I that should be baptized by him.' But Jesus said, 'Let it be.' So John obeyed Jesus and baptized him. He was the first man who obeyed Jesus.

"People began to hear that a man had come to baptize people in order that they might enter into the kingdom of God. Many came to hear him, among them even priests from the temple in Jerusalem.

"We do not know how long John preached. Certainly it was not long. The king of the country had taken as his wife a woman named Herodias, who was his brother Philip's wife, and John the Baptist had told everyone that this was not right. So the king sent a soldier and put him in prison."

A baby begins to cry. The preacher pays no attention. Finally the mother gives the baby her breast and the crying stops.

"The king was not a bad king. John had been put in prison only because he had talked against the king. The king respected him, felt that he was a man of God—perhaps, indeed, loved him. If John had not spoken against him the king himself might have gone to hear his preaching.

"There was a young girl who danced very beautifully. She was the daughter of Herodias. The king was greatly pleased with her dancing, and told her that he would give her a gift. Even if it were half of his kingdom he would give it. The young girl went to her mother and asked her what she should demand. And the mother, very angry because John had spoken against her, said, 'Go and ask for the head of John the Baptist on a platter.' So she went back to the king and asked for John's head. The king was very sad. At first he said he would not do it. 'I will not lay my hand upon a man of God because a child demands it.' But he had sworn to do what she wanted, and he did not want to be false to his oath. So he went to the prison, had John beheaded and presented his head to the young girl on a platter. He was not false to his oath, but he was false to his heart.

"Another time I will speak to you of Herod himself."

Tchu-tchu, the Doctor's dog, comes wandering through the black congregation. He knows he must not approach the Doctor, so he comes and sits beside me, and paws me to get attention.

"While John was in prison Jesus began to preach, and John heard that the man he had baptized was now preaching what he had preached. He heard that Jesus was more powerful than he, that he was curing the sick, that he was healing the poor insane, that many more people came to hear the words of truth than when John himself had preached. So John sent from prison and asked, 'Are you he whom we wait for?' Jesus told John what was happening, and he knew that John would understand. And he told the people that John was the greatest man ever born of woman. He had known that God would come with the kingdom, and that the kingdom of God was near.

"This is the life of John the Baptist. And now who was John the Baptist? John the Baptist was the beginning of the kingdom of God. He was the beginning of the Gospel, because he said that the kingdom of God will now come. The prophets saw the kingdom of God at a distance. They said that the kingdom would some time come. John was the first to say that the kingdom of God is at hand. He was the first to say, 'It is for you to prepare your hearts for the kingdom of God. Work and repent. Prepare your hearts that the kingdom of God may come in your hearts.' This is the eternal gospel, first preached by John. 'The kingdom of God is for all,' he said. It is for you to decide whether you will heed the words of John the Baptist, or just leave the words as words."

What does all this mean to the auditors? I look around me but the dark faces are impassive. The two interpreters give impassioned translations. Schweitzer speaks quietly; they speak with fervent utterance, and their gestures are vigorous. They speak with their whole bodies, not only with their tongues. Do their pagan hearers respond to the words of truth? The faces tell nothing.

"In the words of John the Baptist we have the first fulfillment of the prophets. Three things had been foretold, and here they have come true.

"First, the prophets had promised that God would send a man to prepare hearts for the kingdom of God.

"Second, they had promised that Christ, the Messiah, would come.

"Third, they had promised that God would send his Holy Spirit.

"Here, then, are the three great fulfillments that we should take to our hearts. John the Baptist had been chosen by God to announce his kingdom. So Jesus said that he was the greatest of men.

"The greatest of men! Can you understand what it means when the Lord says of someone that he is the greatest of men? Jesus knew the hearts of men, and he said that John was the greatest of them all.

"When the king of the Galoas lived where the Doctor's house now stands, people said that he was the greatest of men. 'He is like the sun,' they said. But he was not the greatest of men. He had many faults. He was a weak man. He was a man who did badly things that he should have done well. He was a man who had no courage when he should have had courage. 'The greatest of men,' Jesus said, 'is John the Baptist.'

"If there should come a man who was king of all the world—Europe, America, Asia, Africa—he would not be the greatest of men. The true grandeur of a man is to understand the heart of God. John had spoken the words of God when he said that now is the time when the kingdom of God should come. He was greater than any of the prophets because his heart was filled with the spirit of God. The others said that it was still night, and they did not know when the dawn would come. John, in the middle of the night, said, 'The sun will rise.'

"I hope you will also understand who this man was, that every year when the bell sounds for the Feast of John the Baptist you will know that it sounds for the man that Jesus Christ called the greatest of men, that you will try to find the true greatness which was the greatness of John the Baptist. So the will of God will be done in your hearts.

"John was the first to die for the kingdom of God. He went to his death before Jesus went to his death. He was his servant even unto the end."

The simple sermon ends. The final prayer begins.

"O God, we can never thank you enough for the great preacher of the kingdom of God whom you have sent, the man who gave us an example, the man who had strength to put into our hearts, the man who was the servant of God. May he make us the servants of God. We thank you for all the riches that you have put within us. Give us to understand these riches. May we desire to have your strength within us. Give us then the will to be thy children. *Amen!*"

Another hymn is sung, the benediction is quietly spoken. The service is over.

It is still night in Africa, but John the Baptist speaks again. Work, repent, prepare ye; the kingdom of God is at hand.

Epilogue

HE MARCHES ON BEFORE THEM . . .

Out of the jungles of Africa, black and mysterious, he comes. Those who know him and work with him are close behind; but back in the night others come, more and more of them, a growing multitude in endless procession —simple, untutored souls who have been touched by his hands of mercy, blessed by his words of love. Along the tortuous forest trails they come, out of the dark into the light. He marches on before them, with firm and confident step, with clear, unclouded eyes, bringing to us his gifts of vision and devotion. Albert Schweitzer—servant of man and beast, lover of God, humble disciple of Jesus of Nazareth.

Our Task In Colonial Africa

The task of the whites is to make good and worthy people out of the natives, people able to meet as well as possible the exacting conditions in which they have lived since they have been in contact with the outer world—and even to shape these conditions wisely. This work of education is only in its initial stages. It will take time. In order to meet these new demands the native must develop and strengthen certain qualities. Seriousness, faithfulness, sense of responsibility, honesty, trustworthiness, love of work, devotion to the calling in which he is placed, enterprise, prudence in the management of his material welfare, independence—these qualities are what constitute character in the best sense of the term. We, the whites, have won this character in a long development. With the native it will also take generations. And he must achieve this development under much more unfavorable circumstances than those that existed for us.

Normally character is developed by generations engaged in agriculture and handicraft. Both of these activities develop characteristics of worth. The native, however, is prevented from being a farmer or a craftsman as our forefathers were. He does not live in an age of agriculture and handicraft but in an age of industry and world trade—the influence of which stretches over the entire world, even to villages in the jungles and on the steppes. The native has no opportunity to become a real handworker except in special cases. The utensils and products that our forefathers devised and made with the labor of their hands are delivered to him by industry. It is impossible for any handwork to flourish because of this importation of manufactured goods. Even what handwork exists is ruined by it. So the work that is given to the native makes no such demands upon him for planning and for manifold knowledge and skill as the handicrafts would make. It offers him no possibilities for development; it does not inspire in him the same joy of labor. The machine anticipates him in everything: he achieves only a limited, not a perfect, skill.

Conditions in agriculture are similar. It is not possible for the native to be an independent and efficient farmer. The machine takes work away from him. But more than that, he is not allowed to wring many kinds of produce from the earth by diverse skills; rather must he cultivate what the imports permit, what the exports demand. He is condemned to concern himself not with the soil but with plants and plantations. The privilege of being proud of his calling as a tiller of the soil is his only in part, not completely.

Our forefathers formed the fine traits of their character at a time when they were able to lead a quiet and assured existence. Stable conditions virtually guaranteed success to any well-started and well-tended enterprise. A man who was efficient in his work was certain of success. Earnings and savings maintained their value. The development of the natives, on the other hand, takes place in an age when everything is in flux, in a state of transformation and of uncertainty. The conditions necessary for fruitful activity are no longer present. Catastrophes are no longer to be foreseen, ability cannot protect from failure, cleverness is often more successful than worth.

Our forefathers developed in nonpolitical times; the natives must begin their development in political times. It was taken for granted by our forefathers that they would be ruled by persons who in accordance with certain accepted hypotheses deserved to be their masters. To this or that person whom they had elected to be a counselor or official they turned over the conduct of public affairs. This seemed to them even more natural when, in the epoch at the beginning of the modern period—the seventeenth and eighteenth centuries—a ruler appeared who was considered to be stronger than his predecessors in righteousness and good sense. In those times men could live for their work and accumulate their earnings steadily.

Today, when the peoples have taken the conduct of public affairs into their own hands, this peace and unconcern are things of the past. Countries are plunged into constant confusion. Parties fight for power. Individuals can do nothing else but participate in these conflicts—professing certain points of view with like-minded people, contesting against the others.

What emerges from such conflicts as "the will of the people" does not possess the authority required for genuinely effective rule. Statutes and measures are obscure and inappropriate, because they are not carefully considered and quietly worked out with sole concern for the right. They come from compromises upon which people have agreed so far as they could.

The unfavorable circumstances affecting the development of the colonial tribes might have been greatly mitigated, in so far as industrialization and world trade had brought it about. The other consequences of the rule of the people could have been avoided. Rule by the will of the people did not exist among these tribes. It was something unknown to them; it would never have occurred to them to claim it. They might, therefore, have benefited by the experience of our earlier generations. In peaceful and orderly fashion, they might have made spiritual progress through confident submission to the rule of the whites.

But in the First World War the right of the self-determination of peoples was set up as the first objective to be realized. Although it was formulated as a universally valid principle, its applicability to the colonial peoples was not intended. The next step was taken in the Second World War. From that time on the colonial powers were expected to accept as their first aim (and the only one that could be justified) the giving of self-rule to the colonial peoples as soon as possible. It became the duty of the powers to abandon the desire to govern and guide these peoples as before. The new ideal and purpose of the guardians, it was now said, should be to reach as quickly as possible the day when their wards would attain their majority.

The propaganda for this new theory not only intentionally ignored and discredited everything that colonization had contributed, but also proposed to abolish it as something that could never be justified, something displeasing to the idealism of our time. Colonialism was uncritically dismissed as reprehensible "imperialism."

Behind the new theory lay the conviction that the colonial peoples could not progress properly because they were ruled and tutored by strangers, and that only when they became independent could they lead a normal life that favored their development.

It is an unfortunate circumstance in connection with the new theory that it creates at once a false perspective. It pushes to the fore something that belongs in the background. One acquainted with the colonies and well intentioned toward the colonial peoples cannot accept as the first and most important aim that they should achieve independence as quickly as possible—as though this were all that is necessary. The chief goal can only be that they should assimilate under the most favorable conditions whatever in civilization is useful and essential to them, thereby becoming people of real worth and humanity. When they have made this measure of progress, they may then decide whether it is imperative that they should govern themselves. It is, however, in no way useful to their development that they should now be brought to consider their independence as the first essential. To the degree in which their attention is fixed upon this secondary matter they will be diverted from preoccupation with what should really concern them.

Moreover, they are in no way prepared for the manifestations of the will of the people. The whites have fashioned and developed their parliamentary institutions little by little. They possess them as something that has come naturally out of their historical and social evolution. The colonial peoples are not in a position to adopt, as their own, institutions that appeared under entirely different circumstances. The situation is already evident in the fact that the majority of natives, in dealing with ballots, ballot boxes and voting lists, are illiterate. It is necessary for others to mark the candidates for them by different numbers of crosses.

Those who live in colonies that already have come to feel the results of interrogating the will of the people (which is considered so necessary) have a wealth of voting anecdotes which vividly illuminate the extraordinary situation. How could such electors be in a position to comprehend questions pertaining to the well-being of the country? How could they choose a candidate with expert knowledge? What will the parties be like that they will some day develop? The natives have not hitherto felt political passions—the unavoidable consequences of the emergence of political activity. No one can foresee what form these passions will take among the natives, and what the results will be.

Under such circumstances, preoccupation with politics makes a fertile ground for agitators who sow dissension. Recently, in many places, very serious disturbances have occurred, disturbances that could be ended only by a resort to force. The fact that blood once flowed between the white and colored peoples in the period when the whites were taking over the territory has nothing to do with the present relations between them. At that time the subduing of tyrannical chiefs was often beneficial to the natives. In addition, neither the new native generations of natives nor the new generations of whites possess any clear and vivid memory of what happened then.

Now, however, under very different circumstances, blood has flown recently between the white and the colored peoples. Only a man who lives in the colonies can understand what this tragic occurrence may mean for the relations between the two.

And how does the freedom to take their affairs into their own hands—this freedom intended for the natives—look? When one undertakes to define exactly what it will be, one moves in the midst of uncertainties. This is because any freedom granted to the native peoples will always be a limited one. The former colonial districts are not at all capable of economic independence within any foreseeable future. They are not in a position to produce by themselves what is required for economic independence. They have neither the means to create the required equipment nor the organizational capacity to keep production going. On many grounds—and particularly in view of the difficult and complicated economic conditions of the modern world—they need the support and leadership of a greater and more efficient state in all matters of economics. Every effort to make themselves economically independent can only lead to greater subjection to one or more states. Political independence can be conferred upon a people—but economic independence it must win through its own powers.

Colonies can become independent only in the sense of remaining nominally free political creations that belong to the former motherland as members of her empire. This means a more or less far-reaching limitation of their freedom, a limitation in which they voluntarily acquiesce.

It is not easy to formulate this idea of a freedom that limits, and it is exceedingly difficult to realize. For the right to have something to say on economic matters carries with it, among other duties, the duty to maintain the order that is necessary for economic prosperity. The problems of this limited freedom may be concealed in formulas but they may not be done away with. They will give rise to continual conflicts. The natives are inclined, because of the freedom they already have, to take a more complete freedom for granted. They find it hard to understand that only an incomplete freedom can be given them. Therefore they continue to ask in the name of freedom for more than can be granted. A freedom that can only be a limited freedom creates a false situation whose consequences no one can foresee.

Something else must also be taken into consideration. Those who do not know the colonies imagine peoples, all of the same kind, with national aspirations toward independence like those of European peoples. In reality they are tribes that belong together only in so far as they are together subjected to one foreign power and belong alike to one district of government. Those that formerly fought each other are compelled to get along together, and tribal differences are to a certain extent obliterated. With the attainment of independence, however, this unity falls apart. The inevitable consequence is that the tribes again think of themselves as separate tribes, differences come again to light, and the tensions between them acquire new meaning. Those who worked for the freedom of India spoke and acted in the name of the Indian people. They disregarded the fact that there is no Indian people, but only Indian *peoples*. When the liberation took place, that fact—which they tried to ignore—found immediate expression in horrible incidents. The situation in the colonies is similar. Where elections have already been held, old enmities have reappeared, giving a glimpse of what may happen when independence is a fact.

For the colonies to be independent would not mean, then, that they were on the way toward a propitious evolution, but rather that they were on a different path.

Fortunate it is for foreign educators, if they find comprehension in the native world (which is all too much inclined to be attached in these matters to an idealism dominated by modern fictions) of views that correspond to reality and of efforts that conform to reality. But most fortunate of all would be the finding of intelligent natives who perceived what their brothers needed, and co-operated in the educational work designed to produce true worth.

To date there is no comprehension of the concept of a common humanity. The native merely knows that in his own case he is sympathetic with and ready to help only those of his own tribe. With them alone does he feel any kinship. "This is a brother for me," he says of another inmate of the hospital, even though he is related to him in no other way than through membership in the same tribe. This completely primitive way of thinking makes him feel no relationship whatever with those who do not belong to his tribe. To him they are strangers, whom he sees beside him without the slightest feeling that they concern him in any way. The idea of others as fellow human beings does not exist for him. This creates special difficulties for the doctors and nurses. If they call a man to aid in lifting a stretcher on which a sick man lies, he may refuse to help, giving as a self-explanatory justification, "He is not a brother for me." If it is a native just arrived from the interior, no reasoning, no pleading, no threatening, makes any difference. He cannot be altered in his attitude.

If some slightly ill patient should occupy a place next to a bedridden patient who is seriously ill, doctors and nurses cannot rely upon him to perform services that the latter may need in his immovable condition—even when this task has been urged upon him with kindly words of affection. They must find someone who is a member of the sick man's tribe to take the adjoining place.

One of the missionary's greatest tasks is to get the native to give up his idea that members of another tribe are foreigners and to recognize the ties that bind man to man. The parable of the merciful Samaritan takes on a very special meaning in the missionary's preaching.

The first and decisive emancipation in the thinking of the native would be to convert him to the idea of neighborliness and to get him to show it in his relations to strangers. The efforts of the missionaries during long decades in the region of the Ogowe to do something to enlighten and educate the natives in this respect have borne some fruit. The idea of neighborliness has not yet, however, really penetrated the mind of the natives. Even when they are under missionary influence they are in constant danger of falling back into the old ideas, feeling that hostility toward members of another tribe is perfectly natural.

Where the circumstances do not make it easy for the colonial peoples to achieve a superior civilization, there is the danger that they will assimilate the externals of our culture instead of what it possesses of value. The whites who are concerned with the well-being of the natives cannot shut their eyes to this peril. However, they must not let themselves be discouraged by this from carrying on the necessary educational work; they must see that the natives, not satisfied with assimilating the outer trappings of our civilization, will strive to become people of genuine and sterling humanity.

Set in Linotype Caledonia
Format by Robert Cheney
Endpaper map by Miriam Woods